Miracle in Shreveport

Miracle in Shreveport

A MEMOIR OF BASEBALL, FATHERHOOD, AND THE STADIUM THAT LAUNCHED A DREAM

DAVID AND JASON BENHAM

with Tim Ellsworth

W PUBLISHING GROUP

AN IMPRINT OF THOMAS NELSON

Published in Nashville, Tennessee, by W Publishing Group, an imprint of Thomas Nelson.

Published in association with the literary agency of WTA Services, LLC, Franklin, TN.

Thomas Nelson titles may be purchased in bulk for educational, business, fund-raising, or sales promotional use. For information, please e-mail SpecialMarkets@ThomasNelson.com.

ISBN 978-0-7852-1599-8 (eBook)

Library of Congress Cataloging-in-Publication Data

Names: Benham, David, 1975– author. | Benham, Jason, 1975– author.
Title: Miracle in Shreveport : a memoir of baseball, fatherhood, and the stadium that launched a dream / David and Jason Benham.
Description: Nashville, Tennessee : W Publishing Group, 2018.
Identifiers: LCCN 2017037666| ISBN 9780785215981 (hardback) | ISBN 9780785215998 (ebook)
Subjects: LCSH: Benham, David, 1975– | Benham, Jason, 1975– | Baseball players—United States—Biography. | Christian men—United States—Biography. | Christian biography—United States. | Twins—United States—Biography. | Brothers—United States—Biography. | Baseball—Louisiana—Shreveport—History.
Classification: LCC GV865.B37 A3 2018 | DDC 796.357092 [B] —dc23
LC record available at https://lccn.loc.gov/2017037666

To Grampa and Gramma.
Thanks for your faithfulness to come to all
our games through the years. And thanks
for always buying our cleats and gear—
playing in sneakers would've been tough.
Even though you screamed at us from the
stands, we always knew you loved us.

CONTENTS

Introduction ix

1. The Birth of a Dream 1
2. The Stadium off I-20 7
3. Little League Life 15
4 In the News 25
5. A Jailhouse Prayer 33
6. College Days 41
7. Torrington 47
8. Hit-and-Run 57
9. The Draft 67
10. A Red Sox Rookie 77
11. Bluefield Baseball 85
12. Meet Me in St. Louie 95
13. Broken 105
14. Dying to the Dream 113
15. A Summer Visit 121
16. Home Run Derby 127
17. A Crazy Idea 135
18. A New Day 143

CONTENTS

19. Break It Up 151
20. Shreveport 159

Epilogue 169
Appendix: Article from the Dallas Morning News 177
Notes 191
About the Authors 195

INTRODUCTION

God is always at work in our lives. Even when we can't see Him, He's working in ways we may never know. But sometimes we get to see His fingerprints in our life's story firsthand, and it marks us forever. From that day forward we walk with a newfound strength, armed with a testimony of God's goodness, His faithfulness, and His sovereign hand to write *our* story into *His*tory.

John Piper once said, "God is always doing 10,000 things in your life. And you may be aware of three of them."[1] We've found this to be true in our own lives. Maybe you have as well. We all have difficult and trying times when things seem to be going wrong and we can't catch a break. It's just the way of life on this side of eternity. And sometimes we question God or wonder if He really even cares at all.

Well, He cares. We know this because we've been there before. And we've watched Him work in ways we never imagined possible. Many of you know us from the time we got fired by HGTV, which was a tough time for us. We'd thought a new show with a major network was our chance to do something great for God—something that could influence our culture for good. Then the rubber met the road, and we refused to compromise our principles. That's when we got the old heave-ho and lost the show.

Getting thrust into a media controversy was not exactly what we had in mind for our lives. But God was working behind the scenes, and we could trust Him because we had seen Him work on our behalf before. We drew strength from an earlier time where God stepped in, peeled back the curtain, and showed us His divine hand working in a way that blew our minds.

This is that story. Sometimes it's even hard for us to believe—but it's true. We had seen God work in such a powerful way as young Little League baseball players with a dream of making it to the pros one day that regardless of what happened with HGTV, or anything else, we would not be shaken.

The story in this book has brought extraordinary strength to us through the years. We believe it will strengthen you as well. Chances are, you'll see yourself in this story. At some point in your life, maybe you've wondered how God was going to work everything out for you as well. You may even be there right now. Though the details of your story will be different from ours, the fact is that God is the One faithfully writing *your* story into *His*tory.

So come with us as we take you back to a time in our lives when the most important thing in the world to us was the game of baseball.

One

THE BIRTH OF A DREAM

*The one constant through all the years, Ray, has
been baseball. America has rolled by like an army of
steamrollers. It has been erased like a blackboard, rebuilt
and erased again. But baseball has marked the time. This
field, this game: it's a part of our past, Ray. It reminds
us of all that once was good and it could be again.*

—Terence Mann, *Field of Dreams*[1]

I
t was a warm, sunny Saturday afternoon in May 1984. The
days of summer were closing in rapidly, and for two young boys
the thought of no school for three solid months was exhilarating. We had just completed our morning chores—I (Jason) had
mopping and bathroom duty, and David ran the vacuum. (He
always got the easy jobs.)

As we coordinated our teams for another epic Wiffle ball
battle with the neighborhood kids, Dad interrupted us mid-
argument.

"Jason! David! I'm taking you to see a movie today."

Movies were a big deal in the early '80s—some of the greatest flicks of all time came out of that memorable decade. Not to mention some of the most incredible fashion the world has ever seen. Oh, the fashion! We rocked Kaepa shoes, parachute pants, Members Only jackets, neon T-shirts, and Brian Bosworth hairdos. You just don't get any better than that.

So even though we loved playing Wiffle ball, we didn't argue with Dad in the least. We jumped in the car and headed to the Walnut Twin Theatre—the best-kept secret in Garland, Texas. It was the only dollar movie theater around, and since Dad earned a pastor's salary, that's where we typically went.

He took us to see *The Natural*, a movie about a young boy, his dad, and a game that drew them together. It was a movie about baseball, the power of a dream, and the deep bond between a father and his son.

Little did we know the effect this movie would have on us, as it brought to life the very same relationship we had with our dad around the same game.

Roy Hobbs (played by Robert Redford) was a young farm boy with remarkable talent that was hard for his dad to miss. As the two of them played catch in the backyard, his dad said, "You've got a gift, Roy. But it's not enough. You've got to develop yourself. If you rely too much on your own gift, then you'll fail."[2]

That sounded just like our dad. He talked to us the exact same way when we were in our backyard playing catch. He could see we had talent, but he always reminded us that talent was never enough.

Roy and his dad shared a dream together—that one day he would make it to the big leagues and be the greatest player ever.

But before his dad could see this dream come true, he died of a heart attack, right under an old oak tree in front of their little farmhouse.

Now, we must admit, even though we were only nine, we both got choked up pretty good. That's a tough pill for any young boy to swallow. (I think David may have scream-cried in the back row.)

Roy ended up making a bat out of the wood from that tree and went on to pursue his dream—alone. Yet the bond of baseball still drew him close to his father. Ultimately, after taking a few wrong turns along the way, Roy realized his boyhood dream and became one of the game's greatest players. But he did it alone, without the man with whom he longed to share it.

The movie ended with Roy Hobbs, as an older man, playing catch with his son the same way he had with his father.

To say that movie affected us would be an understatement. We walked out of the theater that day with a newfound exuberance for the game of baseball and the hope of one day playing professionally with our dad watching from the stands.

Our dad's love for the game of baseball ran deep. We grew up on his stories of all the Yankee greats—Mickey Mantle, Moose Skowron, Joe DiMaggio, Yogi Berra, and all the legends. He also taught us that true Yankee fans don't like Roger Maris. Still can't quite figure that one out.

His love for baseball, and the Yankees in particular, came as the result of one fantastic day in his life when he was ten. His dad—our grandpa—was a saloon owner in Syracuse, New York. While our dad always believed Grampa to be a good father, our grandpa was also very busy with the saloon and had an affinity for gambling. So he and Dad didn't spend a lot of time together.

But the one thing that drew them together was a mutual love for the game of baseball.

Once, Grampa came home from the saloon in the wee hours of the morning during the school week and woke up our dad. He asked him, "What's the one thing you would like to do more than anything else in the whole world?"

Although caught off guard, Dad responded, "Go to a Yankees game!"

"Then that's exactly what we're going to do," replied Grampa.

Little did Dad know that Grampa had previously made all the arrangements—he already had him excused from school, bought the plane tickets, booked a hotel, and bought game-day tickets to see the 1958 Yankees.

When Dad tells us this story, he still gets choked up. Baseball was something he and Grampa loved together. It was the time when Dad felt closest to him. And while they didn't get to spend as much time together as Dad wanted, on this day everything was perfect.

Dad would replay every little detail of the story to us as boys, especially the moment he and Grampa were decked out in their suits and on the subway from the hotel to the game. As the subway approached the stop, it went up and out of the tunnel. And there, for the very first time, Dad saw the most beautiful sight his little eyes had ever seen: Yankee Stadium.

When they exited the subway, Dad heard the crack of the bat and could smell the popcorn, but, most of all, he could feel the love of his father and the warmth in his heart while holding on to his hand—a moment he and his dad experienced together.

As they neared the stadium, Dad could hear the music playing, and when they got inside, he said he'd never seen grass that green, and the most athletic men he'd ever laid eyes on were taking batting practice in their renowned Yankee pinstripes.

That day gave birth to a deep-rooted love for the game of baseball in our dad's heart. It was a love he was determined to pass down to us.

As we walked out of the movie theater, Dad was wiping tears from his eyes. He willingly admitted he had cried for much of the movie. What we didn't realize then was how deeply this movie affected him as it portrayed a love between a father and his son and how the game of baseball brought them together. Dad saw on the screen what he had shared with his own dad and what he had experienced that day in 1958.

We caught it that day—the very thing our dad had caught at Yankee Stadium—a love for the game of baseball. And on that May afternoon, as the three of us watched *The Natural*, a dream was born—a dream that we all shared together from that day forward. Playing professional baseball was *our* dream—not just for the two of us, but for the three of us: me (Jason), David, and Dad.

We had no clue what God had in store for David and me, but we were armed with a new determination to be the best baseball players we could possibly become. As soon as we got home from the movie, we were in the backyard playing catch with our dad.

We could never have guessed that just a few years later the dream would be refined even more—a dream about baseball, a father and his sons, and a stadium that brought it all together.

Two

THE STADIUM OFF I-20

And there used to be a ballpark
Where the field was warm and green.
And the people played their crazy game
With a joy I'd never seen.

—Frank Sinatra
"There Used to Be a Ballpark"[1]

Today it sits empty and abandoned, infested by bats (the flying kind) and invaded by weeds, just a shell and a memory of the dreams, the energy, and the drama it used to hold. But for twenty-five years, Fair Grounds Field in Shreveport, Louisiana, hosted some of the best of professional baseball around—that is, minor league baseball.

Hot, sticky summer nights. Hot dogs, nachos, and popcorn. Bright lights. Crazy entertainment between innings. Country music and the seventh-inning stretch. And players fueled by the hope of making it to the big leagues, or filled with fear, clinging to one last shot at the dream that had driven them for years.

As Brett Mandel wrote in his book *Minor Players, Major Dreams*, "Minor league baseball is where big dreams meet slim chances and wide-eyed boys develop into big-league men—or hang up the uniform for the last time. In the minor leagues— between the chalk lines, in the uniforms, on the bus trips, and behind clubhouse doors—the magic can be felt."[2]

Minor league baseball is indeed a world unto itself. From the Biscuits of Montgomery and the Flying Squirrels of Richmond, to the Muckdogs of Batavia and the IronPigs of Lehigh Valley, minor league teams are as diverse and colorful as the cities in which they reside. Almost 250 teams make up the Minor League system all across the country and in Mexico, Canada, and the Dominican Republic. With twenty-five players on a team, you're talking about more than six thousand baseball players, all hoping to one day get the call.

And that, at its root, is what minor league baseball is all about. Take away the stadiums, the fans, the nicknames, the lousy food, the long bus rides, and the often horrendous performances of the national anthem (we've heard some crazy ones over the years), and you're left with about six thousand men— some still teenagers, some pushing forty—all chasing their childhood dream.

That's what Fair Grounds Field in Shreveport, Louisiana, represented for us—a dream. It's sad for us to think about the stadium's demise because, for much of our youth, Fair Grounds Field was a thriving stage for our own dream, a dream that strengthened when we were kids during one summer road trip.

Summer Drives to Georgia

It was just before dawn. Jason and I had been up late the night before because excitement about our vacation kept us awake. Think Christmas in July for a couple of spirited young boys, and you get the idea. Dad interrupted our peaceful slumber at 4 a.m., rousing us from our beds and spurring us to get into the car and on the road for the twelve-hour trip along Interstate 20.

"Boys," he whispered, shaking us gently awake. "Jason, David, wake up. It's time to go."

We groggily stumbled out of bed and slowly made our way out of the house.

Growing up in Garland, Texas, as the sons of a pastor, we didn't take elaborate vacations to the beach or the mountains or anywhere, really—other than to Atlanta, Georgia, to visit our mom's family. We spent our vacations there with grandparents, aunts, uncles, and cousins, every July, like clockwork, for almost twenty years. And every single year our dad would make us run the one-mile trek to the top of Stone Mountain. We'd top it off by watching the laser show on the flat side of the mountain that evening. If you need a good taste of the South, just head over to Stone Mountain during a hot summer night and listen to Ray Charles sing "Georgia" over the loudspeakers during the laser light show. It's a beautiful thing.

The bulk of our preparation was completed the night before the big trip. So in the mornings we'd just pack up our 1979 ice-blue Caprice Classic station wagon—a beast of a vehicle. We'd lay the seats down, spread out our sleeping bags in the back (this was before wearing seat belts became mandatory), and place the cooler—loaded with cold Reese's peanut butter cups, M&M's,

and cans of Tab—behind the driver's seat. Dad always took us with him the night before to get the car washed and detailed. That was a big deal for us because it was our cue that the next day our summer trip would begin. Years later, to earn a little spending money while in college, we spent a summer detailing cars. We'd seen the process done to our station wagon enough times that we considered ourselves experts.

We piled into Baby Blue by 4:30 a.m. for our departure. And with $500 in traveler's checks in his pocket, Dad drove. Mom sat shotgun, and we snuggled in sleeping bags in the back, along with our older sister, Tracy. Dad made his way through our neighborhood and headed to I-20, where he picked up speed and settled in for the long trip east. Even now we still can remember the rubber clacking sound that the tires made as we traveled over the regularly spaced seams on the road. We'd drift off to sleep again in the early morning darkness.

About three hours later, as we neared Shreveport, Louisiana, Dad ruffled the tops of our heads.

"Boys," he whispered, trying not to wake up our mom, who was snoozing hard core in the seat next to him. There's nothing like the sight of your mom with her eyes closed, head cocked back, and mouth wide open. You can imagine the fun two twin boys had with that. Fortunately for her, there were no cell phones or social media back then.

"Boys, wake up," Dad said.

The sun had started its ascent by then. We woke up, rubbed our eyes, and saw in the distance where Dad pointed. To us it looked like the Yankee Stadium Dad had told us about in stories of his childhood. It was the biggest stadium we'd ever seen. We hadn't been to a Texas Rangers game at that point in our lives, or any other professional ball game, for that matter. But right off the highway, on the left side of I-20, sat the brand-new Fair Grounds Field.

"That's the Shreveport Captains' baseball stadium," Dad said. "That's where the pros play."

"You mean, like the ones we see on television? The same ones we saw in *The Natural*?"

"They're not in the big leagues yet, but they're pros, for sure—just one phone call away from the majors," Dad explained. "That stadium is where Double-A baseball players play. To get there you have to be drafted by a major league team. And this is where you play to prepare you for the big show."

Directly next door to the new baseball stadium sat Independence Stadium, home of the annual NCAA Independence Bowl football game, on the Louisiana State Fair Grounds. We'd seen that before and were impressed, but the sight of Fair Grounds Field captured our imaginations.

As young little-leaguers with a fresh dream of playing pro ball, the sight of a stadium where professional baseball players competed utterly fascinated us. We began to think of how wonderful it would be to play in a stadium like Fair Grounds Field one day. Maybe we could hit home runs in that stadium, just like Roy Hobbs did. It wouldn't be far from Dad, so he could watch us in person.

"Dad, do you think we could ever play in that stadium one day?"

"You bet you can. I believe in you, and I know the Lord has given you the talent to play the game," Dad told us. "Let's pray that one day God will not only allow both of you to play in that stadium as pros, but together, on the same team."

Passing by the Shreveport Captains' stadium that early morning was when, for the first time, the dream of us playing pro baseball together, at the same time on the same team, was birthed. But Dad didn't just give birth to a new dream in our hearts that day; he also sowed the seeds of earnest prayer to a loving God, teaching us to place our dreams in His hand.

Every summer from that day forward, as we drove down the interstate to visit family in Georgia, we looked forward to seeing the most amazing baseball stadium. Like clockwork, Dad would reach his right hand behind him and ruffle our hair to wake us up. We'd put our hands in his, close our eyes, and he'd pray.

"Lord Jesus, I pray that You would bless my boys. And I pray that one day these two arrows would get to play together in that stadium for Your glory. Amen."

As soon as he said, "Amen," both of us were zonked out again until we woke up at Shoney's on the other side of Shreveport. The restaurant didn't know what hit it as ravenous twin boys annihilated the scrambled eggs, bacon, and grits on the all-you-can-eat breakfast buffet. It was a tradition we looked forward to every year.

After spending two weeks in Georgia, climbing Stone Mountain, playing endless games of Wiffle ball with our cousins, and swimming until our skin shriveled, we'd pile back into Baby Blue and roll through Shreveport again on the way home. This time it was night, and the Captains were playing at home. We'd see the bright lights shining from a long way off, the crammed parking lot, the scoreboard lit up in center field, and we'd feel the adrenaline surging through us as we passed by.

"Boys, look at that!" Dad said. "There it is again! That's what it looks like at game time."

So he'd pray again that God would bless his boys, and that somehow, some way, He might make a way for us to play together at that stadium on the same team for the glory of Jesus.

The prayer was simple and short. But it was one we never forgot. And at that point in our young faith walks, we really had no idea whether God was truly listening.

Three

LITTLE LEAGUE LIFE

Little League baseball is a very good thing
because it keeps the parents off the streets.

—Yogi Berra[1]

By the time we were eleven, we were not only die-hard baseball fans but also blossoming players. Dad was our coach in Little League, and Grampa was the resident "yeller."

"Fire it in there! Just fire the ball!" Grampa would yell if either one of us threw an off-speed pitch to trick hitters into swinging. He hated for us not to use our best weapon—the fastball. Sometimes we'd mow through an entire lineup of hitters before someone made contact. So if we went away from "the heat," Grampa was there to immediately bring us back into line.

"Just give 'em the heat!" he'd yell.

He and Gramma had taken a construction job with JC Penney in Dallas, so they were able to watch most of our baseball games in Little League. Grampa never sat down in the bleachers. He always found a spot away from the crowd where he'd stand and watch. And when he needed to, he'd yell. We knew exactly where he was every game. Interestingly, after we got to college and Dad was no longer our coach, he'd watch our games the exact same way Grampa did. I (David) remember Dad being at one of our games, but I couldn't see him, that is, until I stepped up to the plate and saw him peeking through the bushes in center field as the pitcher was winding up to throw the ball. Yeah, it was pretty distracting.

You know who Grampa *should've* been yelling at back in Little League? His own son, for those crazy-tight coaching shorts, with his socks yanked up to his kneecaps! Dad had his shirt tucked in tight and a fishnet baseball cap propped up nicely on top of his '80s mullet. He was the quintessential 1980s Little League coach.

Our summers growing up were spent primarily on the Little League baseball fields of Texas, with Dad coaching, us playing (eagerly anticipating free snow cones at the concession stand after the game), Grampa yelling, and Mom ringing her famed cowbell. For us, life couldn't get any better until Dad would remind us that dreams don't accomplish themselves. He said we needed discipline to make our dreams a reality.

Turning his teaching into training, Dad signed us up for the Turkey Trot, an annual eight-mile race on Thanksgiving morning in Dallas that drew about twenty thousand people. We'd never run more than a mile before, so this was going to be a real test. Gone were the days of riding our bikes alongside Dad while he ran. It was time to put the bikes away and start running with him.

As race day neared, we were nervous wrecks because Dad threw out a challenge—we had to run all eight miles without stopping. Even during our training with him, we'd never run that far before. So to get motivated before the race, we did what any eleven-year-old boys would do: we watched *Rocky III*.

What affected us most was how Apollo Creed fired up Rocky during his intense training by saying, "No pain!" Rocky echoed, "No pain!" and the grueling work continued.

Dad adopted that mantra for us, calling out, "No pain!" as we ran behind him, and we replied, "No pain!" every time. On race day, Dad pulled us aside for a pep talk.

"No pain, boys!" he said.

"No pain!" we replied.

"All right, Dave and Jase—no matter how bad it hurts, I know you can make it all eight miles. Now, go do it! No pain!"

That "No pain!" cry became our commitment to never stop.

We didn't have running shoes or running shorts, so we ran in MacGregor baseball cleats, vintage '80s knee socks pushed down above our ankles, sweatpants, and long-sleeved white T-shirts because it was so cold. We looked like clowns, and our feet were toast after the race. We'd often take turns leading, drafting off each other as we trudged through mile after mile. Neither one of us would quit because we each knew the other one wasn't going to quit. And that whole thing about "No pain!" became a lie we told ourselves because it often hurt like crazy!

Even with sweatpants and baseball cleats, we ran the whole thing without stopping. It was the first time in our lives we'd ever done anything like that. The rest of that Thanksgiving Day was spent visiting the bathroom, a lot. It's surprising what physical exertion can do to your insides.

The next year Dad signed us up again, and this time on

race day, he decided to step up the game. He handed us white headbands with the word *Jesus* written with red marker on them.

"You boys need to run all eight miles without stopping because you've got Jesus on your heads," he told us.

Seriously, Dad?

Even though we looked like twin Napoleon Dynamites, we ran all eight miles again. Quitting with Jesus strapped across our domes was not an option for us. And for several years after that, until late in our teenage years, we continued to run the Turkey Trot with Dad. Fortunately for us, and for the rest of those who ran the race, Dad's shorts got longer and looser as the years went by.

Signing us up for the Turkey Trot was Dad's way of teaching us that dreams don't just happen—we have to do our part with discipline and let God do His part with blessing, as He sees fit. And discipline comes much easier when you have the luxury of a twin to push you.

We were naturally competitive, but it never led to any kind of jealous rivalry. Our dad saw to that. Dad taught us that competition was meant to build up, not tear down. And the only way this would happen was if we refused to compare ourselves to each other. Rather, we were trained to be content with how God had uniquely gifted each of us. We discovered that comparison breeds either envy or pride—*I'm not as good as him*, so I'm envious, or *I'm better than him*, so I'm proud.

This is the only way we could have made it out of our house without one of us killing the other. Dad and Mom both reminded us that we were on the same team with a common God and common goal—and if we ever lost sight of either one of those, we would end up tearing each other down instead of building each other up. The dream of playing professional baseball was ours together, and tearing each other down would only hinder, not help our journey.

We typically spent several hours every day on a vacant sand-lot with our dad throwing batting practice or hitting ground balls to us. And each time he'd teach us life lessons. The most important one was how to face our fears. Because baseball is a game of inches, even the slightest flinch can cost you the game. An actual baseball is hard and can hurt if you flinch when you're hitting or fielding, so you have to overcome your fear and attack the ball instead of moving away from it.

On one occasion Dad told us to grab our bats and get into the backyard. He was going to teach us a lesson. Our yard was small compared to most, but it was just big enough to have a pitcher's mound and a home plate. Dad usually sat on an egg crate behind the plate and told us to fire the ball as hard as we could. We still remember times we bounced the ball right off his shin—he'd yell at the top of his lungs and hobble around the yard as if he'd stepped on a land mine. The older we got, the worse it hurt. Eventually he made each of us catch for the other while he stood by watching.

But on this particular day the roles were reversed. He was standing on the pitcher's mound with a bucket of tennis balls. He seemed a bit agitated, and as he looked down at his shins, we figured he was holding a grudge.

"One of you get in the batter's box," he said abruptly.

"Uh, what are you going to do?" we asked. David watched while I slowly stepped up to the plate.

We knew our backyard was too small for him to expect us to swing away. But before we said another word, he reared back and threw a tennis ball right at my head.

Thunk! Right off my cranium. The ball bounced into the neighbor's yard while David laughed hysterically.

"What the—?"

Thunk, Thunk, Thunk—my back, hip, and leg all received what felt like 100-mile-per-hour blows from tennis balls.

Mom happened to be watching and yelled out, "Flip! What in the world are you doing? Leave the boys alone!"

"Not now, Faye. I'm teaching these boys to stay in the box even when they're scared. Jason, get back in the box!"

If we didn't stay in the box and take the hit, he would make us stay there until we did.

"Face your fears, boys. If you do it here when nobody is watching, you'll do it in a game when everybody is watching," he told us.

At the time, we thought this lesson was just a sick joke. But it taught us to face our fears of getting hit by the ball. Eventually we got to the point where we never flinched at the plate anymore. (Thank God tennis balls are soft.)

Dad wasn't just concerned with us being the best *players*; he also wanted us to be the best *people*. So as our Little League coach, he came up with two unique ways to teach us how to serve others and honor God through baseball. First, the two of us were in charge of cleaning up the dugout after every game. We may have gotten the game ball, or even at times had the newspaper waiting to interview us, but we weren't allowed to do anything until the dugout was clean. He'd say, "If you want to make it to the big leagues, you've got to be faithful in the little leagues."

Second, we never played on Sundays. He taught us that if we honored God, He would honor us, and choosing to sit on Sundays would teach us to worship God more than we did baseball. As young kids, this one was a tough one, especially since we had to miss several key games, including one championship game.

"God will get you boys right where He wants you to go," Dad would tell us. "All you've got to do is be faithful right now."

While Dad taught us to be faithful as baseball players, we watched him model faithfulness as a father even more. Although he was hard on us in terms of discipline, he was also sure to keep a close relationship with us. Josh McDowell once said, "Rules without relationships lead to rebellion."[2] Two stories stand out that show how our dad modeled this crucial balance.

Each year for Dad's birthday, Gramma and Grampa would buy him a gift. On his fortieth he asked for an Easton Black Magic baseball bat. We were thirteen at the time and desperately needed a new bat, but Dad couldn't afford the one he knew we loved. So, without us knowing, he asked our grandparents for the bat as his gift.

On the day of his birthday, he was out jogging when our grandparents showed up with the bat. We couldn't believe our eyes when they handed it to us. We still remember seeing Dad jogging up the driveway, wearing his baggy shorts and thigh-high grey socks and with his T-shirt in hand, smiling from ear to ear as he saw us holding the bat.

He was so excited, he took it from us, held it up with his arm extended to the sky, and took off running. Up and down the driveway he ran with the bat, as if he had just found a priceless treasure. He then walked over and handed it to us, saying, "This is for you, boys."

That selfless act, where he chose to get *us* something for *his* birthday, spoke volumes. He was willing to sacrifice his desires to give us the tools we needed to pursue our dream.

The other time Dad modeled balance between rules and relationships came in December that year. He woke us up one morning while it was still dark, whispering, "Boys, get up. We're going on a trip."

We had no clue what was going on. All we knew was that we had school that day and that Christmas break was just a few days away.

"We're doing what?" we asked. "Don't we have school?"

"I've got that covered," he responded. "You're going to be with me today. I'm taking you somewhere special."

In the same way Grampa had done back in 1958 for him, Dad had already made arrangements for us to be out of school. A rush of adrenaline shot through our bodies as we jumped out of bed, got changed, and hopped in the car.

For two hours we drove, without Dad even giving us the slightest hint of where we were going. All he said was, "You'll see."

We finally slowed to a stop in a tiny Texas town. As we pulled up to the stop sign, Dad said, "Do you see that sign over there?" He pointed to a sign that read, "Nocona, Texas—Leather Goods Center of the Southwest."

"We're in Nocona, Texas, where some of the best baseball gloves in America are made. I've worked it out with their factory to give us a behind-the-scenes look at how their gloves are handcrafted."

"No way!" we said, thinking this was the greatest gift he could have given us. By this time in our lives, we were playing a lot of baseball, and the cheap Kmart gloves just weren't cutting it anymore. We needed good leather gloves, but we knew they were too expensive.

For the next several hours the three of us were like kids in a candy store. We watched every part of the process—from cutting out the imprint from a piece of rawhide, all the way to the final touch of branding the name Nokona on the gloves (we never figured out why they replaced the *c* with a *k*). We even saw their one-of-a-kind *glove-breaker-inner*—an older man with a hand of steel who would put a glove on and whack it violently with a wooden mallet. We shook his hand just to see if it was real.

We got to the end of our tour and fully expected to go home with two new baseball gloves, but that's not what happened. We got in the car feeling a little dejected.

David finally spoke up. "Hey, Dad, do you think we'll be able to get a glove like that one day?"

"I don't know, bud. You know how expensive those things are," he responded. "Let's pray and ask God to make it possible."

A few weeks later, on Christmas morning, after we had just finished unwrapping all our gifts, Dad came out of his room holding two boxes in his hand. He told us to open them at the same time. We ripped them open, and there they were, two brand-new Nokona baseball gloves—the very ones we had tried on at the manufacturer.

Dad said he had been saving up for months for them, and when he took us down to Nocona, he picked them up without us knowing. We have no clue how he slipped that past us, but it was the best surprise we had ever gotten. For the remaining years of Little League, all the way through high school, those gloves were our most prized possessions.

Four

IN THE NEWS

*Baseball is the only field of endeavor where
a man can succeed three out of ten times
and be considered a good performer.*

—Ted Williams[1]

The years brought more family trips down I-20 for our annual summer vacation. The breakfast pit stops at the Shreveport Shoney's didn't stop. Neither did the prayers as we passed Fair Grounds Field. On the way to Atlanta, and on the way home, Dad would pray, continuing to ask the Lord to make a way for us to play together in that stadium, and continuing to stoke in us the dream of doing so. As we got older, sometimes Dad asked us to pray instead of him. We always obliged, often fighting over which one was going to do it.

At times we kicked around the idea of stopping in Shreveport to see the stadium more closely, maybe even to watch a game if the Captains were in town. But we never did. And the older we got, the more that decision became deliberate. We decided we wanted the first time we set foot in the stadium to be when we were playing there.

Before that could happen, though, we had to make baseball our top priority athletically, and for a while, it lost the battle to other sports. During junior high and early in our high school years, football and basketball captured our affections more than baseball did.

We attended a public school during grade school, but for junior high our parents moved us to Garland Christian Academy (GCA), where our sister, Tracy, was already a student. As eighth graders, we were featured in *Sports Illustrated*'s "Faces in the Crowd" section in May 1990 for football and basketball. Baseball legend Ken Griffey Jr. graced the cover of that issue, the first time for him to do so. Inside, *SI* told of how we as eighth graders had led GCA to district championships in football (with a 10-0 record) and in basketball (at 18-1):

> Jason, a tailback, rushed for 1,111 yards and 10 touchdowns and threw six TD passes. On the court, where he played guard, he shot 56% and averaged 17 points and 3.1 assists a game. David, a quarterback, threw for 1,498 yards and 19 touchdowns and then, as a basketball guard, shot 62% from the field and averaged 13.4 points and 3.6 assists.[2]

Next to the write-up were our two smiling faces.

The beauty of this story, however, lies not in the fact that we were featured in this magazine, but in the title on the cover. Hovering over Ken Griffey Jr.'s picture were two words—*The Natural.* A gentle reminder of the dream we shared with our dad.

While we excelled in and loved basketball and football, the older we got, the more baseball gained ground. The nostalgia we felt with baseball and the dream we shared with our dad was a powerful attraction. Basketball and football didn't quite have that. We loved baseball because our dad loved baseball and because Grampa loved baseball.

Over time it became increasingly clear that baseball was where we had a greater chance to excel at the next level. And for us, that next step was going to be college, not the pros. Although in baseball you can play professionally right out of high school, our parents wanted us to have more time to mature before we landed in that environment.

We hoped we would get college scholarships for football and basketball. But for baseball, we *knew* we could get college scholarships *and* have a chance to play professionally.

So we began to concentrate on baseball more and more, and by the time we were juniors in high school, it was our primary focus. But GCA, with only 176 students in high school, didn't have a home baseball field, so every game we played was an away game. And our practice field was the corner of our football field. We knew we were going to have to work hard to get noticed.

For a time the three of us—Dad, David, and I (Jason)—thought long and hard about going to a public school, where we could get more looks from college and pro scouts. The pressure of getting full-ride scholarships was heavy on us, as we felt it was the only way we could play at the next level. A pastor's salary of $18,000 a year wouldn't make a dent in college tuition for two boys.

But Mom would have none of it. She told us to bloom where we were planted. Dad ultimately came around to her way of thinking, which was always a good idea for him. They must have talked quite a bit about it because Dad found a new fervor to encourage the two of us to be faithful right where God had placed us.

"God loves impossible situations," he would tell us. "It gives Him a chance to show off."

Now, you have to remember—we played back in the days before the Internet and social media. And one of the main ways scouts learned about up-and-coming athletes was to read about them in newspapers or magazine articles. The key for us was to play well enough to be noticed by them and, hopefully, make it in.

It took some time, but by the time we headed into our senior year of high school, we started to see momentum. *Collegiate Baseball Newspaper* listed us in June 1993, along with two other sets of twins, as "Amazing High School Twins." The whole *twin* thing worked to get us noticed. Being a twin was outside our control, but it's one of the first things publications started noticing. Fist bump to God Almighty for that one!

During our junior year, David hit .442, and I hit .431, with six homers apiece. A few months later the same publication included us among their "Top Prospects," and Mizuno named us to their All-American team after our senior year. By God's grace we played well enough in high school to be named All-District four times and also named to the All-State and All-American teams. God was promoting us as we advanced toward our dream.

But there was one major bump in the road along the way—a twist that caused a major setback early in high school and almost caused us to lose sight of the dream.

It was during our sophomore year, near the end of baseball

season. I was shagging fly balls in the outfield with the guys on an overcast day. It had rained pretty hard the day before, so the grass was still damp. Our coach was hitting us fly balls when I noticed another ball lying on the ground. Without hesitation I grabbed it and threw it as hard as I could to second base.

The minute I let go of the ball, it felt as though a lightning bolt had hit my right shoulder. I could barely lift my arm. The pain was excruciating.

Like a moron, I had picked up a water-logged ball, which is a few ounces heavier than a normal one. All baseball players know the surefire way to injure your throwing arm is to throw a water-logged ball as hard as you can. And *that* is exactly what I did, injuring my rotator cuff.

Fortunately we had only a few games left, so I was able to be a designated hitter. But I couldn't play the field. And for our summer league team, I spent most of the season riding the bench—a place with which I was not familiar nor with which I was the least bit comfortable.

There's nothing like a young man losing the one thing he loves more than anything. Dad and Mom hurt for me. David did too. This was our first real trial in sports. Dad reminded me that strength only comes through strain and that God is able to take our foolish decisions and turn them into testimonies that bring Him glory. But it still hurt, bad.

Although I learned a lot during this time, I didn't discover the real impact until after I was fully recovered in the fall of my junior year. David and I were out in the field playing catch together, and, as usual, we ended our session with a round of long toss (where we throw the ball really far to each other to strengthen our arms). David whisked the ball on a rope to me as I stood about two hundred feet away. I caught it and threw it back—only my ball dropped at the end and bounced to him.

I remember thinking, *Oh Lord, please, no. Please don't let my arm become average.*

David and I were known for our really good arms, and certainly David's was living up to the hype. But now my arm was different—it didn't have the same pop it once had. The more I threw the ball, the more my fear became reality. My arm wasn't the same as it once was.

It was a tough pill for me to swallow, especially when scouts started paying more attention to David than they did to me.

On two occasions it hit home even harder. The first was when I read a scouting report from the New York Mets, who called us in for a private tryout during our senior year of high school. They rated players on a scale between 10 and 60. David's arm: 60. My arm: 30.

The second was in a public tryout for the Atlanta Braves. About two hundred guys showed up for the tryout, and at the end of the day, they lined everybody up and gave them numbers. The head scout then called out about twenty numbers. David's number was called. Mine was not. He then said, "If I didn't call your number, you're dismissed."

Ouch. David was advancing toward our dream. I was not.

Thankfully, I had Dad to walk with me through this tough time in my life, reminding me that God was up to something, and that no matter what, He would make a way. He encouraged me to trust the Lord for a scholarship and to trust Him for the pros.

In the meantime, he encouraged me to be happy for David and not fall prey to comparison. If I did, it would ruin the experience for David. Again, these were tough lessons to learn, but Dad regularly encouraged me with Lamentations 3:27, "It is good for a man to bear the yoke while he is young." This felt like such a heavy yoke.

Instead of retreating into self-pity, I used the injury as motivation to work even harder at baseball. Every day when we'd get home from practice or a game, I'd go by myself to the local elementary school down the road. It had a large brick gymnasium, where I'd stand outside and throw ball after ball at the wall, fielding the ball as it bounced back to me and throwing it against the wall again. One hundred eighty grounders altogether, every day, like clockwork. I knew if my arm wouldn't dazzle the scouts, then my glove, along with my bat, could.

Scouts and coaches love players who can hit even if they have other areas that aren't so hot. And that's something both of us, by God's grace, were able to do. As the stats piled up during our senior year, we began to get serious looks from colleges. We had plenty of smaller schools show interest, several wanting us for basketball and baseball. But we had a strong desire to play for a Division I school, so we weren't really interested in those. A few state schools, like Georgia Tech and Wichita State, had expressed a hint of interest in us, but they weren't offering full scholarships. Without full rides, we weren't going anywhere.

As we prayed earnestly about where to play college ball, we felt God wanted us to attend a Christian university. But it still had to be NCAA Division I ("D-I"). That narrowed our choices to only a few schools, and with us playing for such a small school, like GCA, we weren't on any of their radars. Not to mention the fact that few college teams ever give out full-ride scholarships for baseball.

If our dream of playing pro baseball together was going to come true, we knew the first step was to play collegiately. But the improbability of us getting full rides to a D-I Christian university made it clear we needed a miracle.

Five

A JAILHOUSE PRAYER

God does nothing except in response to believing prayer.

—John Wesley[1]

We owe our college education and college baseball careers to our dad being in the slammer.

That's right. While we were growing up, our dad, Flip Benham, was one of the national leaders for the pro-life movement. He regularly got hauled off to jail for ministering at abortion clinics. This was back in the day when ministry at abortion clinics was met with stiff resistance. Quite often we'd see Dad speaking to a couple seeking an abortion, when the authorities would show up and haul him off to jail. It was a shock the first time, but pretty soon it got to be just a normal thing for our family.

One time, while locked up, Dad was watching TV in his cell, and he came across *The Old Time Gospel Hour*, where he heard Jerry Falwell talking about Liberty University in Lynchburg,

Virginia. We'd been praying about Christian colleges with base-ball programs, and although Dad knew a little bit about Liberty, he had no idea it was an NCAA Division I school. His heart leapt out of his chest as he watched Dr. Falwell brag on the Flames playing Georgia Tech in the NCAA regional baseball tournament. There in his cell, Dad began to pray.

"God, would You please make a way for my boys to play at Liberty? We can't pay for it. We can't afford it. Will You please give them full scholarships to play at this school?"

Such were his prayers, similar to those about us playing together at the stadium in Shreveport—specific and passion-ate. Almost every day, even after he got out of jail, Dad would pray for God to open a door for us to go to Liberty. It weighed heavy on his heart, as he knew that apart from a miracle it could never happen.

He began talking to his friends and anyone with whom he came in contact, telling them about Liberty and how much he wanted us to play baseball there. But he didn't have any idea how to get the coach to notice us.

That is, until Dr. Alan Streett showed up.

Dr. Streett, who knew about Dad's pro-life work, was a pastor of a local church in Dallas. His son, Aaron, had recently joined our high school team, so Alan began watching us play every day. Having previously been a coach and a scout, he knew how to assess players according to the Major League scouting categories—hitting, hitting for power, throwing, defense, and speed—and he determined we had the skills necessary to play professional baseball. So he began writing letters on our behalf. One of his letters was to Johnny Hunton, Liberty's head base-ball coach.

"Last fall I wrote you about my plans to put together a Christian baseball team from the north central Texas area," Alan wrote in one letter. "I also agreed to provide you with any top-notch prospects I felt could help the Flames ball club. Having seen hundreds of players, I am now ready to offer you the two best of the bunch.

"David and Jason Benham are twins," he continued. "Both are juniors at Garland Christian Academy outside Dallas. They are not only top college prospects but now possess the ability to be playing Single-A ball."

Alan told Coach Hunton how we were "on-fire believers" who wanted to play baseball for the glory of God. "As a former professional scout and college coach, I can assure you these two guys are the cream of the crop," Alan wrote.

He also wrote letters to us, encouraging us to work hard and trust the Lord's plans for baseball. It's amazing how much of an impact letters of encouragement can be. But it's even more amazing how God brings certain people our way at certain times in our lives when we need them the most. We still have Dr. Streett's letters.

Due to Alan's influence and some recent articles about us in the news, Coach Hunton decided to make a trip to Texas to watch us play in the spring of 1994. He even stayed with us for three days. He told us later that he wanted to get a good feel for who we were off the field as well as on the field.

He went to church with us, ate with us, watched us work out, even hung out with us and our friends—he was like a part of the family for three entire days. He even fell asleep at the lunch table after church. I (David) will never forget how embarrassing it was when Jason looked over at him and said, "Need a nap there, Coach?" Jason's never been scared to say what everyone else is thinking.

One of the games he watched was against Trinity Christian, the top team in the state at the time. Jason was the slotted starting pitcher.

Yep, I was. And I specifically remember asking God to help me throw well, and hard.

Trinity threw a lefty that day, and several scouts were there to watch. By God's grace, David and I both played well—well enough that a few scouts talked with us after the game. Coach Hunton had to wait to greet us after the scouts left. The Lord had crafted it perfectly.

As soon as we arrived back at our house with Coach Hunton, he asked if we could take a seat in the living room—the two of us, our mom, and our little brother and sister. Dad was out of town at a pro-life event that day.

"I've seen a lot of baseball in my day, and the level of play I saw today was some of the best high school baseball I've seen. If you boys can play at this level, you can certainly play at the next. But what I like best is the leadership you both exhibit off the field, and that's something our team could really use," he said.

At this point it seemed as though the words were coming out of his mouth in slow motion. Was he going to make us an offer or what?!

As we sat there for what seemed like forever, he then pulled out two letters of intent, pushed them across our coffee table with a pen, and said, "I would like to offer you both full-ride scholarships to play baseball at Liberty University."

Boom!

The Lord had answered Dad's prayer. From a jailhouse petition to full scholarships—the Lord had moved on our behalf. We were totally dependent on God to provide for us, and when there was no way we could have played for a school like Liberty apart from divine intervention, He stepped up and knocked it out of the park—for us.

As Coach Hunton left our house that day, I caught a glimpse of his notepad—the one he had written on during our game. The top edge of it was sticking out of his bag, and what I saw confirmed even more that God was behind this. I saw my name with a scribbled note next to it, "Jason—Good arm."

Only God.

Before we took off for Virginia to start our collegiate careers at Liberty, we still had to finish high school and deal with the Major League draft in June. While David had a good feeling he could get drafted, I was still holding on to the hope that I could as well. But it was highly unlikely either of us would have bailed on Liberty and gone the professional route because we knew our parents wanted us to go to college. Still, it was fun to think about.

That May, in 1994, the New York Mets held a predraft camp in Dallas, and we were invited to work out along with three other guys. As we mentioned previously, after the workout they asked the other players and me to leave but kept David to work out some more.

"David, we heard you do some catching," they told me.

"Well, yeah, every once in a while," I said.

They told me to get behind the dish. So there I was, behind

the plate, with them throwing me pitches and timing my release on throws to second base. My times were good—1.74 seconds, 1.72 seconds—which were faster times than some major-leaguers.

"If we draft you, will you sign?" they asked me.

"I don't know," I said. "Draft me, and we'll see." (I've always been a better negotiator than Jason.)

A few days later, during the draft, I got a call from the Mets, telling me that they had selected me. It was an awesome feeling. A major league team liked me enough to give me a chance to play for them. Even though I knew I probably wasn't going to sign with them, what eighteen-year-old baseball player wouldn't want to be selected in the draft?

My joy was short-lived, however, because Jason didn't get a call. The surreal feeling I had lasted only those two days of the draft. When it was over and Jason wasn't selected, my joy ended as well.

I (Jason) knew that I probably wouldn't get selected in the draft, but in the back of my mind, I was holding out hope that maybe, just maybe, some team would want me too. It's hard not to get excited about a possibility like that even if you know it's a slim chance. So I checked the full draft list in the Sunday paper, that hope evaporating as I passed over round after round of names without finding mine.

I was happy for David, but I sat in church that day and cried for two hours straight. It seems silly now because we were planning to go to college even if both of us had been drafted. But that was the first time I realized that maybe my dream of playing professional baseball with my brother might not come true. I was a good baseball player, but David was better. While I wanted him to succeed, I wanted desperately to succeed right alongside him.

My tears in church that day made David cry as well. What a sight we were—a couple of athletes with full scholarships to play Division I baseball, crying in church. There David was, drafted by the New York Mets, but in tears because his twin brother wasn't drafted as well.

It shows the kind of relationship we had. When you've worked so hard with someone else and suffered together to achieve a goal, and he doesn't experience the same blessings as you, it actually diminishes your own blessing—because your thoughts aren't about you but about him. He may be a doofus a lot of the time, but I knew his heart was hurting for me.

Since I (David) wasn't drafted in the first few rounds, I never even considered signing with the Mets. For starters, I knew I wasn't high on the organization's priority list. I may have gotten a small signing bonus, if that, but it wouldn't have been enough. More important, though, was that I wanted to go to college with Jason. Baseball was our dream together. It was never an individual dream. Getting drafted by the Mets made me excited for about five minutes, but that excitement quickly faded when Jason didn't get the call.

After the drama of the draft receded, we spent the rest of that summer looking forward to the next chapter of our lives, which was about to begin at Liberty. In August we loaded up our parents' Dodge Omni sedan—the same ice-blue color as that Caprice station wagon from our childhood—with a little

U-Haul trailer attached to the back, and headed east along the familiar I-20 toward Lynchburg, leaving our Texas home behind us.

About three hours into our trip, we passed Fair Grounds Field in Shreveport. We paused to pray again, as we had been doing for years. And every summer and winter after, like clockwork, for the four years of driving to and from Liberty, we passed by that stadium and prayed that we would get there—holding on to the dream we shared together.

Six

COLLEGE DAYS

Every strike brings me closer to the next home run.

—Babe Ruth[1]

We left for Liberty for the first time in the summer of 1994. We weren't boys anymore. We were men. But that didn't stop us from getting Zack Morris (from *Saved by the Bell*) haircuts just before hitting campus. I (David) remember we also made the decision to read through the Bible every year while there—a habit we still have to this day.

Gas was $1.11, stamps were $.29, and "I Swear" by All-4-One was the #1 song that year. But the most important fact from 1994 was that our beloved Dallas Cowboys won the Super Bowl. The only problem for us was that the World Series was canceled because of a players' strike.

When we arrived at Liberty, we were blown away by how blue the Blue Ridge Mountains were. It never dawned on us before we arrived in Lynchburg that that's why they were named that way. As soon as we hit the baseball field, we prayed about two main goals. The first was to win a game in the NCAA regional tournament. This is where the top forty-eight teams in the nation compete for a chance to play in the College World Series. At this point, Liberty had never won a game in an NCAA regional tournament—in any sport. The second was for both of us to get drafted.

My path to the big leagues as a catcher was much easier than Jason's. Quality catchers are in high demand in professional baseball. I felt I'd probably get drafted again after my junior year at Liberty, and again after my senior year as well. Jason, however, was a shortstop, and he didn't fit the mold for the prototypical big-leaguer. Middle infielders typically need to be short and quick, and Jason was tall and lanky.

"Lord, I don't know how this is going to work out for Jason," I'd pray. "He's going to need a miracle, and I know You can make that happen." (Jason: Man, you make it sound like I was brutal. I just got a full ride to a D-I school!)

Fortunately for us, we landed starting positions our freshman year of college—me as catcher and Jason at third base. Our whole family came out to see us that first year. As usual, Dad found a special spot to watch the game, all alone. Our little brother and sister came along, and Mom brought her cowbell. Our grandparents came as well. We didn't pitch anymore, so we never got to hear Grampa yell, "Fire it in there!" But then, he wasn't quite as energetic as he used to be either.

While it took time to get acclimated to our new positions, we both played well. As a freshman, I was even named to the Big South All-Conference team, which was a big deal for a first-year player.

Just before our sophomore season started, we got a call from Dad telling us Grampa wasn't doing too well. We quickly hopped on a plane and flew out to visit him.

Dad rarely missed a baseball game of ours—from Little League all the way through high school. And on game days when Dad was in the slammer, Grampa and Gramma would always be there to watch us play. They didn't like to sit down during games, so they'd both stand up the whole time, pacing and yelling (or as they liked to call it, "cheering").

Every season Grampa and Gramma would buy us baseball cleats and a bat. They were fully vested in our success as baseball players. Grampa used to collect all his loose change for a week and then exchange it for rolls of quarters. He'd give them to us so we could go down to Twin Rivers batting cages and hit off the batting machines, often tagging along with us. He used to say, "Just watch the ball and swing hard, boys."

But now cancer had gotten the best of him, and when we arrived at his bedside, he was a shell of the man he once was. The once-vibrant businessman with a deep love for his family and the game of baseball was now on his last leg and wanted to say goodbye to his grandkids.

We knelt down next to his bed and just sat there, fighting back the tears. We didn't know what to say. What words could we find to say to the man who had poured so much into us? I then said, "Grampa, maybe one day we'll get drafted by the Yankees and play in Yankee Stadium."

We weren't sure he could hear us or comprehend what we were saying, until he turned his head slowly toward us and whispered three words, "Any big show." These were the last words Grampa ever said to us. *Any big show.*

Two days later he died.

We wanted more than anything to have our dad in the stands to watch us play pro ball one day, and we wanted Grampa there too. But God wanted him home.

Those three words carried more weight than anything else he could've said. *Any big show.* The particular show didn't matter—what mattered to Grampa was that we had a goal, pursued it, and accomplished it, and that he was able to be a part of it. He was proud of us for the way we'd worked so hard to earn college scholarships, and it was his joy to see that dream come to fulfillment. But the dream of playing pro ball would have to continue without him.

After saying our final goodbye to Grampa, we returned to Liberty for our second season, with David continuing to excel on the diamond. He had a great sophomore season, while I turned in another average year. For college players, hitting .300 is rarely good enough to get drafted. And for some odd reason I struggled to get over that mark.

While David may have had an advantage over me on the field, he was no match for me when it came to being the responsible one. He would've never made it through college if I hadn't been there. Ask him—he'll willingly admit that, if he's honest with himself.

We owned an old white Isuzu pickup truck together, but he never had his own set of keys—I wouldn't allow him. He'd lose them the minute he got them. And he was such a lightweight that he couldn't drive early in the morning or late at night, so I was the one who assumed that responsibility. I don't know how he's able even now to drive his family places.

On one of our road trips heading back to Liberty after Christmas break, we left at our typical 4:30 a.m. All David said to me was, "Wake me up when we get to Shreveport," before he zonked out and lay there unconscious for three hours.

We finally rolled into Shreveport.

"Dude, wake up," I said. "There's the stadium. Let's pray."

"You pray," he replied, wiping the drool off his shoulder with his eyes still closed.

By then, I was fighting to stay awake, so when we were done praying, and against my better judgment, I told David he needed to drive. Just outside of Shreveport, I pulled over and made him take a couple of laps around the truck to wake up. He jumped behind the wheel while I settled in for a quick nap.

Ten minutes later, rocks started hitting the side of the truck.

Startled awake, I saw David in the driver's seat, hand on the steering wheel, head cocked back, mouth open wide, sound asleep. Even worse, we were headed right for the median.

"David!" I yelled.

"Whuaahh!" he said as he reacted.

Of course, when you're startled awake like that, you tend to overreact. And that's exactly what he did. As we headed for the median, he jerked the steering wheel, and we did a 720 back across the highway. It felt like slow motion as I yelled at him for being so stupid (I've since repented of the things I said that day). By God's grace there were no cars around us, so we didn't get hit, nor did we flip the truck, but we did slide down into a ravine on the other side of the highway and stopped, literally, about two inches from a tree.

"Are you kidding me?! I drove three hours to Shreveport, and you couldn't drive ten minutes!" I scolded.

"What the heck, Jason?! You know I'm not good at driving in the morning . . . or evening. Chill out!" he barked back.

After a few minutes of collecting ourselves and making sure our pants weren't soiled, we got out and tried to get the truck back up the hill and onto the highway. But no luck—we were stuck. Fighting back the temptation to punch David in the face, I decided we needed to pray. We didn't have cell phones, so we had no other options for help. We decided to climb to the top of the hill and back to the highway to try and flag someone down. Within thirty minutes a tow truck saw us and pulled over to the shoulder. He used a winch to lift us up the hill and back onto the road. Less than an hour later we were back on the road. David was in the passenger seat—for good as far as I was concerned.

Throughout college we had plenty of memories driving past Fair Grounds Field in Shreveport and praying together, but none of them topped that one.

Praising God that we were still alive, we returned to Liberty for our junior year, with David turning in another stellar season on the field. Thankfully, his baseball skills were not affected by his horrific driving. That year only widened the gap between the two of us on the field. Something had to change for me, and it had to change quickly. My whole family had been praying earnestly for a couple of years now that God would bless me and help me develop as a player. They had no idea how their prayers were about to be answered.

Seven

TORRINGTON

A good coach can change a game; a
great coach can change a life.

—John Wooden[1]

At Liberty I was having a hard time getting attention as a player. I was good enough to keep my starting position, but I just couldn't turn in high enough numbers to stand out in our conference, much less for big-league scouts. David had no problem, as he was named All-Conference again after his junior year and continued getting noticed by Major League teams. The more we played, the more I realized time was running out. I only had one more season to make an impression—a big enough one to get drafted and keep our dream alive.

This is what the summer of 1997 just after our junior year represented for me—one last opportunity to improve my swing and turn some heads.

Wood Bat League

Players typically use the summer to work on aspects of their game that need fine-tuning, and for college athletes there are plenty of summer leagues to choose from. They're called "wood bat summer leagues" because the players use wood bats to hit so scouts can tell how well they will adjust to the professional game. Succeeding in a wood bat league is a significant stride toward getting drafted. And there's no better preparation for Minor League life than playing collegiate summer league baseball—the long bus rides, cheap hotels, dusty sandlots, and bad food—all the things that make an unforgettable summer for a baseball player.

The previous summer, after our sophomore season, we traveled overseas with Athletes in Action, a division of Campus Crusade for Christ. While we had a deep love for baseball and truly enjoyed playing collegiately, God had been working on our hearts, showing us that there was more to life than the game of baseball. He began to reveal to us that His desire extended beyond putting up good numbers, getting drafted, or even pursuing the dream of one day playing in Shreveport. We started to feel an even stronger burden to use the game of baseball to tell people about Jesus—to use our ability in the game we loved to tell about the One we loved.

So after our junior year at Liberty, we planned to spend another summer traveling with AIA, but a team in the New England Collegiate Baseball League (NECBL)—the Torrington Twisters—called and invited both of us to come up to Connecticut to play with them for the summer. This was a wood bat league and would be a great opportunity for us. But after we prayed about the decision and talked to our dad, we decided to return to AIA. The reason? We felt that's where the ministry opportunities were.

Knowing we had to deliver the bad news to the Torrington general manager, we went into our dorm room at Liberty and made the call. But the moment we hung up the phone, we both felt sick to our stomachs—like a deep gut-ache that told us we had made the wrong decision. Before the call we'd felt like we were doing the right thing, but afterward we both just sat there in a dazed silence.

David finally broke the silence and asked, "Did we just do the right thing?"

We both agreed to pray again. As we knelt down beside our beds and asked God to give us guidance, we felt a gentle nudge from the Holy Spirit.

David said, "For some crazy reason I really think we're supposed to go to Torrington."

"I do too," I said. "Let's call him back right now."

When the general manager picked up the phone, he was shocked to hear from us. "We know you're going to think we're crazy," David said, "but is it too late for us to still play for you? When we hung up the phone with you, we felt we'd made the wrong decision and are wondering if you still want us to play."

"Are you kidding me?" the GM replied. "Of course I do— welcome to the Torrington Twisters!"

We had no idea what the Lord had in store for us there, and we'd almost messed it all up. But God was directing our steps, as He had something "up His sleeve" for us in Torrington.

A few days later the spring semester ended, and we packed our bags and headed from Lynchburg up to Torrington. After arriving, I (David) was notified by the Mets that they had drafted me again. But I was selected later than I thought I would be. I'd had a monster year at Liberty (.384 batting average) and was one of the top-hitting catchers in the country. I had hired an agent, and the dollar figures he threw around to teams scared the snot out of them. So I dropped in the draft.

Jason, meanwhile, was overlooked again. His junior season at Liberty was decent (he hit .308), but it wasn't good enough to draw the attention of the big-league scouts. In fact, during his junior year, Jason started making plans for life after baseball. He actually began studying for the law school acceptance test and was thinking about a career in law as plan B. (Jason: That was such a brutal time in my life.)

I refused the offer from the Mets as Jason and I settled in with a host family in Torrington. This small New England town of thirty-five thousand was thrilled about the new team, as player after player arrived and began working out at Fuessenich Park. And the players were excited about being in Torrington as well because every one of them had the same dream we did—play well enough to get drafted.

Jason knew if he didn't improve drastically, he'd lose his chance at the draft. It was his final chance to establish himself as a big-league prospect.

Enter Coach Greg Morhardt. Everyone called him "Mo." He was the team's hitting coach who had a reputation that preceded him. At one time he'd been the hitting coach at Liberty and was a legend for his success with hitters. Some players called him the "Yoda" of hitting coaches, while others referred to him as Roy Hobbs from *The Natural*. We had heard about him before, how, still in his midthirties, he could launch balls over the wall and knew how to train college hitters to do the same, but he left

Liberty before we got there. So we were thrilled to find out he lived in Torrington and was coaching the Twisters.

The impact he had on us, especially Jason, was nothing short of miraculous.

Coach Mo

And a miracle was exactly what I (Jason) needed. Just so you can get a gauge for the type of baseball guy Mo was, years after Torrington, he became a Major League scout and was the guy who discovered and signed Angels outfielder and two-time MVP Mike Trout, arguably the best player of his generation. He convinced the Angels to take a chance on Trout in the first round of the 2009 draft, and now they have Mo to thank for it.

But that was still years away from the summer of 1997. Mo had recently left his assistant coaching position at Liberty because he needed to make more money to support his family. He returned to his hometown in Connecticut and took a job working in a group home while he went back to school to finish his college degree. The Twisters found out Mo was back home, and with the team starting up, they hired him to be the team's hitting coach.

During our first practice, Mo watched me taking batting practice. "Jason," he said, "you're missing the bat cock."

"Huh?" was my bewildered response.

"Your bat's flat," Mo explained. "You're not getting any rhythm with your hands. If you were to grab a whip, how would you swing it?"

I drew my hand back and made a whipping motion in the air.

"That's it," he said. "Now, just do that with the bat."

"Oh," I replied, as if he had just shown me a treasure map. "That's it?"

"Hitting is all about timing and using your hands properly," he continued. "That's why you can have these scrawny guys who look like they've never lifted a weight in their lives excel as hitters, while players who are physical specimens can languish and never develop at the plate. Hitting isn't about strength. It's about your hands," he explained.

As much as I would love to say my strength was the issue, it turned out I wasn't using my hands properly. At Liberty, the more I struggled with hitting, the more I began to tighten my grip on the bat and use strength to hit. But a good swing needs to be natural with loose and flowing hands gliding through the hitting zone (where you make contact with the ball). I had over-analyzed my swing so much, trying harder and harder every day to hit better, that I had lost my natural swing.

That summer Mo taught me to swing like a kid again, with no worries or concerns—just loose hands and a smile on my face. He taught me things I'd never been taught before. The only problem was that things got worse before they got better—a lot worse. Everything felt backward, and the harder I tried, the worse it got. For the first fifteen games of the season, I was one of the worst hitters on the team, and probably even the league. But Mo kept encouraging me to trust him, so I stuck with it (even though at times I wanted to snap my bat in half).

Then one day in Middletown, Connecticut, as we were taking batting practice before the game, the switch flipped. All of a sudden, the bat felt different in my hands. I was launching the ball out of the park with unbelievable ease. I felt as if I was barely swinging the bat, while the ball exploded off the bat in a way I had never seen before. And I was swinging with wood!

I remember Mo standing outside the cage watching, and after three or four straight home runs, I looked over at him, and he just smiled. "See? I told you you'd get it!"

By the end of the season, I had finished in the league's top-ten hitters and was selected for the NECBL All-Star team. For the first time in a long time, my batting average was actually higher than David's (although he tied for the league lead in home runs and was named the NECBL's Player of the Year—he was always trying to one-up me).

I remember calling Dad and saying, "Dad! I got it! I got my swing back, and I'm killing the ball. Everything Mo taught me is actually working."

He responded in typical Dad-like fashion, "Buddy, Mom and I have been praying for you. In the same way God brought Dr. Streett into our lives to get you to Liberty, God brought Mo into your life to get your swing back."

Dad wasn't the only one praying for Jason. I was praying too. Watching Jason rip the cover off the ball was as fun for me as it was for him. At the start of the season, I was hitting fourth, and Jason was hitting seventh or eighth. By the end of the year, Jason was up to third in the batting order, right in front of me, like it used to be back in Little League. I couldn't believe what I was seeing. I felt, for the first time in a while, that maybe Jason had a shot at the pros.

As for me, although I had already turned down the Mets,

with the way I played that summer, John Barr, the Mets scouting director, told me they really wanted to sign me: "What's it going to take?" he asked me. "We know you slid late in the draft, but we're willing to pay you."

Those words were enough to get my attention. For the first time, I seriously considered forgoing my final year at Liberty and signing a professional contract. If they were willing to pay some big bucks, then I was going to listen.

The very next day the Mets fired Barr and brought in a whole new regime—new scouting director, new priorities, new direction. The new folks didn't have the same kind of interest in me that Barr did, so the contract talk just wilted, and that was the end of it. God made it quite obvious He wanted Jason and me back at Liberty for our senior season.

Last Game with the Twisters

Our Twisters team finished the season in first place. When it came time for the playoffs, we drew home field advantage, and with the stands packed to overflowing, they announced the starting lineups. Unbeknownst to the fans, we had decided before the game to switch jerseys for the introductions. I (Jason) put on the catcher's gear with David's uniform, and when they introduced him, I ran out crazy bowlegged, as if I had just gotten off a horse, and had my pants hiked up to my chest. The place rolled in laughter. That one felt good.

But the joy of roasting David was short-lived, until the announcer called out *my* name. When David emerged from the dugout, he gently strolled toward the baseline and abruptly fell flat on his face, wallowing around on the ground like a newborn giraffe. The fans erupted. It's the only time David has ever outperformed me in a prank.

We ended up making it to the championship game, but we lost (because David left too many runners on base). But it was a summer that changed my life forever—not just because I found my swing, but, even more important, I had also found the woman who would eventually become my wife.

The chaplain of our team quickly became a favorite among the guys, and when I met his beautiful daughter, Tori, I was smitten right away. Though we weren't married until years later, had the Lord never directed us to Connecticut for the summer, I wouldn't have found my swing, and I wouldn't have found my bride.

We left Torrington with my confidence soaring. I felt comfortable at the plate again, and it had been a long time since I could say that. We were itching to get back to Lynchburg for our senior season at Liberty. We still had the dream before us of playing professional baseball together, and with the strides I'd made in Torrington, that dream was more realistic than it had ever been before.

HIT-AND-RUN

*There are three types of baseball players: those
who make it happen, those who watch it happen,
and those who wonder what happened.*

—Tommy Lasorda[1]

You should have seen the look on our coaches' faces the first time I (Jason) took batting practice at Liberty the fall of our senior year after I'd found my swing at Torrington.

"What's gotten into you?" our hitting coach asked.

"I found my mojo!" I replied.

For the next few months, during fall intra-squad games, I ripped the cover off the ball and landed second in the batting order for the opening of the spring season.

Now, I can't take all the credit here. David had been praying earnestly that God would give me a supernatural senior year. He even prayed that God would take away some points from *his* batting average to add to mine if it would help me have a successful season. I bet he wishes he'd never prayed that last part because God answered his prayer! His batting average slid several points that year.

After spending a few days back home in Texas for Christmas break, we loaded up our white Isuzu pickup at the customary 4:30 a.m. and headed down the road for our last trip to Lynchburg as LU baseball players. This time, as we passed Shreveport, our dream of playing there together seemed closer than it ever had. We were still riding a wave of momentum from our summer in Torrington.

Shreveport Prayer

We prayed, as we always did, not just citing miracles recorded in the Bible, but miracles we had seen in our own lives. "Lord, You've done incredible things for us in recent days," David prayed. "This is getting real now. We want to play together in that stadium. We don't know how You're going to do it, but we pray that You would somehow work in our lives to make that possible."

I chimed in. "Oh, and one last thing—thank You *so much* for giving me a new swing."

We still had a goal of delivering Liberty its first ever win in the NCAA regional tournament. That had been our goal from the beginning, and now we had one last shot to make it happen. Fortunately for us, we were not the only two players who drastically improved over the summer. Our team was finally in a position to make a good run for the conference title and a shot at the College World Series.

Okay, I just have to pause here for a moment. Even as I

reflect back on that senior year, I get goose bumps. God answered all of our prayers in a big way. From my very first game that year up until the last game of the regular season, I was a different player—a completely different player. By the end of the regular season, I had hit more than 100 points higher than in all three of my previous years in college, ending with a .426 batting average. I was selected not only First-Team All-Conference, but I was also named the Conference Player of the Year. To top it off, I was nominated GE Academic All-American for superior performance on the field and in the classroom. Never before in my life had I experienced success like this.

A line from the movie *Chariots of Fire* gives the best description of what I felt on the field that year. Eric Liddell, the famous Scottish Olympic runner, was speaking to his sister about his love for the Lord and his ability as a runner, when he said, "I believe God made me for a purpose, but He also made me fast! And when I run I feel His pleasure."[2]

All season long, the moment I'd stepped into the batter's box, I'd feel God's pleasure. I cannot overstate how amazing this was. It was as if God Himself was inside me, guiding my hands through the hitting zone, crushing pitch after pitch.

It reminded me of a story our dad told us as kids about a dream he had when he was a boy. He was at Yankee Stadium, wearing the pinstripes, when the coach asked him to get into the batter's box to hit against Goose Gossage, the best pitcher of that time. Dad was scared to death and knew he was going to strike out. But just before he stepped to the plate, Reggie Jackson walked out from the dugout and looked straight at Dad.

The beauty of a dream is that *anything* is possible. That look from Reggie Jackson said it all. Stunned, Dad looked down at his chest and saw a zipper. He unzipped it, and Reggie stepped inside. Everything changed for Dad in that moment—he wasn't timid anymore and had a boost of confidence like he'd never felt. On the first pitch he crushed the ball over the outfield wall.

I know it's a crazy dream, but that is what I felt like at the plate. God's presence was so powerful when I was in the box that often after I laced the ball over the fence or delivered one of my many game-winning hits that year, I retreated behind the dugout to pray—and cry. I couldn't help it.

I remember praying, "God, why are You doing this for me? I don't deserve it. You've changed me completely." The feeling of gratitude was overwhelming. By the end of the regular season, I was not only the top hitter in our league but among the best hitters in the nation.

Only God.

The Game Against George Mason

One particular game against George Mason University captured what that season was like in a nutshell. GMU was throwing a lefty who was a top prospect, and as we got off the bus, we could see a line of scouts against the fence, waiting to see him pitch. We'd had scouts at our games before but never this many. Typically they'd talk to David and a few of the other guys afterward, leaving their business cards with them.

But for this game, they were there for the pitcher. We don't remember his name, but he was a major talent, pumping heat at 94 to 95 miles per hour. There were probably fifteen or twenty scouts there that day, and they clearly liked what they saw from this guy who was lighting up their radar guns.

When our leadoff hitter stepped up to the plate, I was in the on-deck circle. I prayed, "God, help me to impress these scouts. Please!"

Although this dude had a fantastic arm, he did not have much control. He walked our leadoff guy, so now it was my turn. I stepped into the batter's box, a left-handed hitter facing a tough southpaw. For those who might not be die-hard baseball fans, left-handed hitters typically don't fare well against left-handed pitchers. I'd been hitting left-handed ever since I was seven years old. Our Little League coach couldn't tell us apart, so he told me to hit lefty so he'd know the difference between us. I hit better from the left side than I did as a righty, which is why I just stuck with it and never looked back.

As I dug into the batter's box, our coach gave me the hit-and-run sign. *Are you kidding me?* I thought to myself. *On the first pitch?* I was itching to get in there and find a pitch to drive, but with the hit-and-run on, my job changed. Now, instead of finding a good pitch to hit, I had to swing at whatever he threw me. Since the runner was stealing second base, my main task was to make contact and get him to third. A swing and a miss would leave him exposed on the base paths, so I had to make contact no matter what.

That's a lot of baseball to digest, but suffice it to say I wasn't going to have the opportunity to show off my new swing to all these scouts. Our coach's plan was in place, and I had to fol-low it.

When the pitcher picked up his leg, I saw our runner take off from first. The pitch came in, a high inside fastball. Letter high, probably six inches away from my chest, at about 95 miles per hour. I tried to swing down on the ball to keep it on the ground, but I turned on the pitch and rocketed a missile over the right field fence. It was an absolute bomb. My attempt at a ground ball turned into a two-run home run.

I pretty much sprinted around the bases. I was so pumped about what had just happened I couldn't slow down. After crossing the plate and getting smacked around by my teammates, I could feel every single scout staring at me, writing my number down, trying to figure out what they had just witnessed. I sat down on the bench, shaking. I'd never hit a home run on a pitch like that in my life—a 95-mile-per-hour, chest-high fastball . . . from a lefty!

While everyone else was looking at me in astonishment, I had an unmistakable sense of what God had just done. When I'd stepped into the batter's box, I'd had a plan. My coach had had a different plan. But God had His own plan, and He'd walked me right into the very scenario that would get every scout in the stands to notice me.

David played well that game too. After the game the scouts stuck around to talk to both of us. Finally, we were both talking with scouts at the same time. It felt so good to be in those shoes. I got a lot of business cards that day, and we both knew what we were dealing with—the chances of us getting drafted together in June were going up quickly.

But before that, we had other business to attend to—namely, getting a win for Liberty in the NCAA Regional Tournament. By God's grace, we won the Big South title (beating Coastal

Carolina), which earned us a spot in the regional tournament. Our team watched in expectation as we gathered together for the ESPN selection show. There we were, on the big screen—Liberty University was headed to the Atlantic II Regional in Tallahassee, Florida. We told this story in our book *Whatever the Cost*, and since it's such a significant part of our baseball journey, we think it's worth retelling.

We faced top-seeded Florida State in the opening round of the regional, and the Seminoles got lucky and beat us 10-7. Actually, it wasn't luck, as they were an awesome team, advancing to the College World Series that year. The loss dropped us into the loser's bracket, where we had third-seeded Auburn in a do-or-die game. This was our last chance to get Liberty the regional win that we had been striving for since we arrived in Lynchburg four years earlier.

Auburn led 2-0 in the seventh when we scored twice to tie the game. With the score still tied in the top of the ninth, Auburn had a man on second base with two outs when their hitter dribbled a routine grounder to third that should have ended the inning. Our third baseman, however, channeled his inner Bill Buckner as the ball scooted between his legs (you'll have to google that name). The problem was, I was that third baseman. Our left fielder couldn't get to the ball in time to throw out the base runner, who scored to give Auburn a 3-2 lead.

I was crushed as I returned to the dugout after we got the final out, but I had a feeling of what God was up to—He was going to allow me to come up to bat with the bases loaded and win the game for us.

Sure enough, we had the bases loaded with two outs, down

by a run, when I stepped to the plate with a chance at redemption. I'd delivered game-winning hits so many times that year, and I just knew that I was going to come through again in dramatic fashion. The catcher and umpire must have thought I was crazy as I was talking in the batter's box: "It's just You and me, Jesus. Just You and me."

A game-winning hit would have been the fairy-tale ending, but on this day it was not to be. I grounded out weakly to end the game. Game over. Season over. College career over. All year I had found a way to come through when the game was on the line and deliver the game-winning hit, but when my team needed me the most, I failed.

In the press conference that followed, with tears in my eyes, I talked to several sports reporters about how important my faith in God was and how I trusted Him even when He didn't give me what I wanted most. I knew I needed to give God praise whether in victory or defeat. Strangely enough, I felt God's presence with me during that moment of defeat even more powerfully than I had all year when He was giving me such great success.

It turns out my words that day had a profound effect on a lot of those sportswriters. John Nogowski, writing in the *Tallahassee Democrat* the next week about the role of faith in sports, reported:

> It seems the media's unofficial but universal philosophy is: Religion is a private matter, people don't want to hear somebody's testimony, just tell us about the home run, stick to the facts, etc. So we do.
>
> But on Friday afternoon, when I sat across from Liberty

College's Jason Benham and listened to his emotional testimony, rivulets of tears rolling down either side of his face as he talked about his faith and his error in the bottom of the ninth that cost Liberty the game, I pondered that old question that you can find on a bracelet on the counter of any Hallmark store: What Would Jesus Do?

The first time I saw those, I told the saleswoman I thought the first thing Jesus would do was not sell cheesy bracelets in card stores.

But as Benham kept talking, I truly did wonder.

"Some day, I may have a son," Benham said. "And if this ever happens to him, I can tell him how his dad cost his team a game but that it's OK. He is all that matters."

Now Liberty University is run by Jerry Falwell, so the religious bent didn't surprise me. But Benham's sincerity did. He went on to talk more about his faith, how he was sure Jesus wasn't going to let him down in the ninth inning when he came up with a chance to win the game.[3]

And Jesus didn't let me down. It wasn't the outcome I'd wanted, but God knows better than we do what we need. In that moment I was simply trusting in His unseen hand.

"By the end of Benham's talk, we were all choked up," Nogowski continued. "Sportswriters generally are a hardhearted bunch with a dim view of mystical things. We look for the wisecrack. But the true measure of Benham's faith was so real, it hit us all."[4]

With a period on our senior season, one dream of ours was dead. We would not deliver Liberty's first regional win. But we had seen something remarkable happen nonetheless. I turned in the best season of my life—bigger and better than I ever could have imagined.

The Lord had answered David's prayers on my behalf in a big way. Now, as we looked forward to the Major League draft a few days after graduation, the question loomed: Was it enough?

Nine

THE DRAFT

*I was a last round draft pick. Nobody wanted
me. I could count the amount of scouts that
told me to go to school, to forget baseball.*

—**Mike Piazza, 2016 Baseball Hall of Fame inductee**[1]

It's not quite the spectacle the NFL and NBA drafts are—prime-time TV coverage, thousands of fans in attendance, and mock drafts by expert analysts. But the Major League Baseball draft is a huge deal for players like us who cling to hope that some big-league team will want them. It was our Super Bowl and World Series wrapped up into one.

The 1998 draft wasn't as big a deal for me as it was for Jason because I'd been drafted twice before and knew I was going to be drafted again. But there was still suspense. What round will I be taken in? What team will select me? Is it going to be the Mets again? After the heartbreak of the regional tournament and the end of our collegiate baseball careers, the hope of getting drafted pulled us through that tough time.

The added suspense this year was whether Jason would be drafted with me. He had a monster senior year at Liberty—a better year than me, in fact, for the first time in a long time. The *Dallas Morning News* even picked up on that, publishing a huge story about us that covered two full pages in a Sunday edition in early June. They had written about us in high school and watched our story unfold, so they flew into Lynchburg to write a follow-up feature article on the local baseball twins from Garland.

Their writer and photographer spent several days with us at Liberty before the NCAA regionals, and then they flew to Florida to be with us during the tournament. They were with us in the hotel, in the locker room, in the gym, at the stadium. Everywhere. They even ran a half-page photo of us kneeling by our beds in our hotel room, praying together after the Florida State game and before the Auburn game.

In our minds they were writing about two brothers from Texas who shared a dream about baseball and were soon to go separate ways in hopes of pursuing careers in professional baseball. But then the Auburn game happened, and the article came out with the headline "Second Nature: Jason Benham Has Accepted Living in Baseball Shadow of Twin, David." It opened with these words:

> Every day, for 22 years, you wake up in a room with him. He looks like you, talks like you, thinks like you. Even friends can't always tell you apart. Until you get on a baseball field, that is, and then it's obvious.

He's better than you.

Not a little better. A lot better. The pros drafted him, not you, and you sat in church and cried. Two years later, they drafted him again and passed on you again. It still hurt, but you were resigned to it.

You had to be. Even after this season at Liberty University, when you outplayed your brother for the first time in your life, when you were the MVP of the Big South Conference, even then you didn't forget who was really better.

You don't forget if you're Jason Benham. Not if your twin brother, David, is one of the best college catchers in the country.[2]

Needless to say, that was *not* the opening we were expecting nor the angle we thought they were going to take. Jason literally laughed out loud when he read this part:

You were good, but he was better, at everything. He is two minutes older, an inch taller, two-tenths of a grade point smarter.[3]

"Better 'at everything'?" he scoffed. "The list of things I can do better than you is longer than Superman's cape. Driving being one of them!" Then he proceeded to remind me that in the Bible, when it comes to twins, the younger is often blessed more than the older. Remember Jacob and Esau? And Ephraim and Manasseh?[4]

I had hoped the article would put us on equal footing, especially considering the year Jason had just had, but that's not what happened.

Even though it started out a little rocky, the article in its entirety portrayed a surprisingly accurate picture of our relationship and the separation we were soon to face. As the writer watched our last game together against Auburn, he closed out the article with these words:

> Baseball still doesn't hold them as equals, but the dream runs on. Only now, as they give chase on those early-morning runs, all each will hear in the stillness is a solitary set of footsteps. It will take some getting used to, closing out 22 years and 1,500 games. After the last one, David got an idea of what it will be like as he walked off the field, his head swinging from side to side.
>
> "Where'd Jason go?" he wondered aloud, probably not for the last time.[5]

Drafted!

As June 2–3, the dates for the draft, grew closer, we headed to Orlando to join our parents at a pro-life gathering Dad had coordinated. By the time we got there, he was already in jail (par for the course). When we talked to him on the phone, he told us how hard he was praying for the draft. Even while he was locked up, it was all he was thinking about—this was his dream too.

We knew I would get drafted, and some had speculated that I might go early. The problem was, as seniors, we knew we wouldn't get a ton of signing bonus money, no matter where we were picked. Senior signs are notoriously cheap because college seniors don't have any leverage. Of course they're going to sign.

What are they going to do, hold out and go work construction for a few months until a team comes to its senses and ponies up more money? A high school senior can always threaten to go to college instead of sign (like I did after my senior year). A college junior can always threaten to go back to school for one more year (also, like I did). But a college senior? The pro teams know they have you, so you're not going to get a ton of cash.

The Detroit Tigers called me in my hotel room the morning of the draft's first day, which made me think I was going to get picked in the early rounds. But I made a horrible mistake. When they asked what it was going to take to sign me, I responded, "Fair money for the round where you draft me."

That was the wrong answer. Fair money for the first few rounds was several hundred thousand dollars, and they weren't about to pay me that much money. I should have told them just to draft me and that we'd work it out. Live and learn.

After I hung up the phone, Jason and I decided to go work out at the gym, which was our typical morning routine. We hadn't heard anything from any other teams that morning, so, still clinging to the hope of a call, we headed to the gym. On the way there and on the way back, we prayed together, asking God to allow us both to get drafted.

When we got back to the hotel after our workout, Mom came running out to the truck. "David, the Red Sox just drafted you," she told us. "They drafted you in the twelfth round." Although it wasn't in the top five rounds, as I had hoped, I was thankful to have been selected and looked forward to finally playing professionally.

But since Jason still had not received a call, I put my prayers for him into hyperdrive.

"Thank You, Lord, for letting me get drafted. But please, God, please let Jason get drafted too," I prayed. "Whatever it takes. Let him get drafted."

Then we started the waiting game. The minutes passed slowly in the hotel as we sat there, anxiously hoping that the phone would ring with news about Jason's selection. But the rest of the day, silence.

We were there in Orlando with lots of folks from the pro-life community who were like family to us. They were very much invested in our success. We had a church service that night, and though people were happy for me, nobody was in much of a celebrative mood because they all were on pins and needles waiting to see what would happen with Jason.

By this time everyone had joined in prayer. "Lord, please . . ."

The morning broke the next day, the final day of the draft. We grabbed breakfast and hung around the hotel for a while, going later than usual to the gym for our workout, hoping the phone would ring. Before we left, we gave Mom strict instructions to sit by the phone in the hotel to wait for a call.

David had gotten his call and was pretty relaxed, but my stomach was in knots as I struggled through the reps, hoping I'd get a phone call from a team—any team. It didn't matter where; it didn't matter what round. All I wanted was to get drafted. It's a very surreal feeling when you place all your hope in God to answer a lifelong prayer. I felt close to Him. I had done my part, and now I had to rely on Him to do His, whatever that meant.

I don't remember what time it was when we got back to the hotel. All I remember is seeing a lot of people congregating outside in the parking lot. When Mom saw us, she darted toward our truck with her hand in the air, waving a little piece of yellow paper. "Jason! Jason! The Orioles called! You've been drafted by the Orioles!"

I went numb. "You're not joking, are you?" I asked. Mom has never been the kidder, but I had to make sure.

"No!" she replied. "I just talked to the scout on the phone, and he wants to talk to you right now."

No way.

I looked at the paper she handed me, and I saw in her handwriting—Baltimore Orioles, 37th Round, Marc Tramuta.

David chimed in, "Dude! Call him!"

We walked into the hotel room with my emotions still in check—I just had to hear it from the Orioles' scout himself before I'd fully believe it. I called the number on the paper, and what I heard next sounded like an angelic affirmation from heaven—"Jason, welcome to the Baltimore Orioles."

The minute I hung up the phone, I ran outside about a block away from the hotel, found some bushes I could hide behind, and got down on my knees with my hands extended to heaven. I began to cry as I prayed, "God, You did it! Thank You so much. I don't deserve this. I love You. Thank You, thank You, thank You."

A dream I had pursued for so long—and had to die to along the way—was now a reality. Though David and I weren't going to the same team and though we wouldn't be playing together, our dream of doing so remained alive.

It didn't take long for us to sign with the teams that drafted us. We stayed in Orlando for several days after the draft until the time came for us each to head to mini-camp with our respective teams. Mini-camp for the Baltimore Orioles was in Sarasota, Florida, while the Boston mini-camp was in Fort Myers, about seventy-five miles south of Sarasota. For the first time in our lives, we were going in different directions.

Separate Ways

It's hard to describe exactly what that was like. For twenty-two years we had done everything together. Everything. We played on the same teams. We slept in the same room. We went to the same classes. We had the same friends. We drove the same car. We were rarely apart from each other for more than a few hours at a time. And now we were preparing for our lives to go in completely different directions.

We didn't have cell phones at that time, and we didn't have e-mail addresses. We knew we weren't going to be in regular communication with each other.

We drove from Orlando to Sarasota and met a friend and former Liberty teammate at a Cracker Barrel there. He lived in Fort Myers, so David was going to stay with him. After we smashed a couple of big Country Boy breakfasts, we headed to the parking lot, and that's when it set in for the first time. We weren't emotional about it, of course. But it definitely was a weird feeling when it came time to say goodbye.

Our paths had been united for our entire lives up until that point. I think there was a part of each of us that, while we didn't want to separate, knew we were following the Lord's direction in our lives. We prayed together in the parking lot that day before we parted ways, that God would be glorified in our lives, and that He would somehow allow us to play together again. "Well, swing hard in case you hit it. See ya around." That was probably about the extent of our farewell.

We thought about Shreveport, and we knew neither the Red Sox nor the Orioles had a team that played in the Texas League, where the Captains played. So while we didn't give up on that dream, we really just moved it to the back of our minds. We accepted this path that God had set before us, and we trusted His will to be done. We had both been drafted, and we were at peace. We were eager to see what we could do on our own and excited to see what God had in store for us as we began our careers as professional baseball players.

Ten

A RED SOX ROOKIE

This Red Sox. Is this a Communist organization?

—**Fidel Castro**[1]

At this point, our stories diverge for the first time in our lives. Jason may have needed a soft blanket and teddy bear for comfort, but I remained strong. After going our separate ways in the Cracker Barrel parking lot, I reported to Fort Myers for Red Sox mini-camp. All the new signees were there, guys hailing from UCLA, LSU, and Wichita State to Puerto Rico, Venezuela, and Cuba—the best baseball players the Sox could sign landed in Fort Myers to train together after the draft.

Now, *that* was an experience. As we received all our Red Sox gear—hats, jerseys, pants, cleats, and bats—none of us showed much emotion. We tried to play it cool. But deep down we were all like little kids. The excitement of being professional baseball players was hard to hide. But when we got out on the field, my excitement turned into determination. I'd be left in the dust if I didn't work harder than ever.

The only problem was that I had never played in 97-degree heat with 100 percent humidity before. It felt like 120 degrees on the field. I'll never forget how hot that first game was. We played the Minnesota Twins, and I was behind the plate. After the first inning I took off my chest protector in the dugout, and it was dripping with sweat. My whole body was so wet that by the third inning, when the runner on first tried stealing second base, the ball slipped out of my soaked hand and rolled to the shortstop. Not the first impression I wanted to make.

But I played well enough during the two-week mini-camp to get promoted to the Lowell Spinners in Lowell, Massachusetts—a team in the New York–Penn League. It was an answer to prayer because the stadium was only a hundred miles away from Portland, Maine, where my fiancée, Lori, lived. I thanked God I wasn't drafted by a team out west somewhere. But even as awesome as it was to have my soon-to-be bride so close to me, Minor League life wasn't nearly as exciting as I'd imagined.

Reality Hits

I discovered rapidly that the *idea* of playing professionally was quite a bit different from the *reality* of it. Jason had the same experience. It's something every professional baseball player has to endure because there's no getting to the big leagues without first traveling through the Minor League. The typical minor league season consists of 140 games in 150 days, not including spring training, so you can imagine how tiring a schedule like that can be.

The first time reality hit was when I arrived in Lowell, and the team gave me a key to my room—in the dormitory across the street at the local university. No air-conditioning. Cheap plastic mattresses. I couldn't sleep because I was so hot, and I didn't have the time or transportation to buy a fan for my room (I gave Jason the truck back at Cracker Barrel because I'm so generous). Those hot nights in the dorm were miserable. Even worse was that the Red Sox took $200 out of our $850 paycheck each month for housing. I wasn't even a real estate agent yet, but I knew we were getting a raw deal.

After taking out taxes along with all the fees, my first paycheck was a few hundred bucks, which was all I had to live on every two weeks. Because I was saving for the wedding, I literally survived on canned tuna and pineapple. It wouldn't have been so bad if the food spread in the clubhouse had been better. Instead, our spread for every game consisted of a gallon tub of Jif peanut butter with a wooden tongue depressor stabbed into it, a dry loaf of white bread, and Smucker's jelly with hardened bread crumbs spread across the top. A few apples and bananas, and that was it—every day. I ate it because it was free and because doing so meant I wouldn't have to spend my paycheck on food. I dropped almost ten pounds that summer. My abs felt great though.

You know it's bad when the best day of your life in the minor leagues is when you're getting on the bus for a six-day road trip and they give you $120 in cash—$20 a day for meal money. If I played my cards right, I could pocket $60. I spent much of my time on the long bus rides daydreaming about the good ol' days back at Liberty, eating all the cafeteria food I wanted. I repented to God for complaining about it so much when I was there.

One day our manager told us to get to the park early the next day to pick up our bonus checks. That was a big deal. As a twelfth-round pick and a college senior with no leverage to negotiate, I had gotten a whopping $4,000 bonus. Some of the earlier draft picks, on the other hand, got just a wee bit more. One of our top picks that year had just arrived to the team, and he and I went together to get our checks. We walked outside together, holding them in sealed envelopes. We decided to open them at the same time.

I opened mine, and I was ecstatic: $4,000 at one time was more money than I had ever seen. I was so thankful, I couldn't stop smiling, and I knew that money was going right into the bank to start my life with Lori in just a few months. My gratitude quickly turned to amazement as my teammate opened his envelope. I had never seen that many zeroes on a paycheck before. The temptation to compare his check with mine was strong, but Dad's lessons about the danger of comparison and the value of contentment echoed in my mind. Dad probably thought I never listened, but I'm glad I did.

My first season as a pro finally ended. It was the longest summer of my life because I was to be married just two days after the last game of the season. I couldn't wait, and since Portland, Maine, was so close to Lowell, Dad got permission from Mom to come early and watch me play a few games before the wedding. As I expected, Dad didn't sit in the seats the team had reserved for him. He simply got his ticket and proceeded to a private spot to stand and watch. There were thousands of people at the game, so to this day I have no clue where he went. He reminded me of Grampa.

On our way up to Portland after the last game, Dad mentioned that Jason's season was extended for a few days, and he wouldn't be able to make the wedding.

"Seriously, Dad? He's not going to make the wedding? He's my best man," I said.

"Bud, Jeets [Dad's nickname for Jason] tried his best. He just can't make it," he replied.

That really stunk because we hadn't seen each other since the Cracker Barrel parking lot, and as hard as it is to admit, I was really bummed he couldn't make it. I know—it's weird. I feel odd even writing that. When we arrived in Portland, all of my closest college friends were there to celebrate with us along with my entire family, except Jason.

The Wedding

That night at the rehearsal dinner, Dad stood up and began to speak. He talked about how amazing my fiancée, Lori, was and the gratitude he and Mom felt about welcoming her into our family. He then began reminiscing about me growing up, how Jason and I were like two peas in a pod. With each story he told, the more my heart felt wrenched. Lori was sitting next to me, with her hand on my shoulder. She knew this was difficult for me.

That's when it happened.

Mom jumped out of her seat and screamed, "Jason!"

Everyone in the room turned around to see Jason walking in

the back door. I still can't believe I'm writing like this, as if he's some superhero or something. But there he was. No one could believe it. Dad was the only one in the room who knew he was on his way. (Jason: I was able to convince my manager to let me skip the last game of the season to be there, but I didn't tell anyone except my dad. So it's his fault no one knew.)

I was sitting with the bridal party, and as Jason made his way to the front, I broke down. I can't remember a single time I hugged my brother in our first twenty-two years together, but on this night we broke our unwritten rule. There we were, in the middle of the restaurant, hugging it out. No words—just crying like babies. (Jason: I can't wait until this chapter is over.) Everyone in the room was bawling. My rehearsal dinner had turned into one massive boo-hoo fest.

While Jason may have stolen the show at the rehearsal dinner, the next day was all Lori. She was absolutely stunning—*Brides* magazine should have been there to capture this breathtaking moment. When she walked down the aisle, it was hard for me to believe she was actually choosing to be mine. After saying "I do," we danced late into the Maine fall night with our college buddies, family, and friends. We then spent a whopping forty-eight hours at a local bed-and-breakfast for our honeymoon. The Red Sox had invited me to the fall instructional league in Fort Myers, which was huge for my career, as teams only invite a certain number of players to participate in additional training for the fall. But it meant our honeymoon would be cut short. That's the price you pay for a chance at the big leagues.

As soon as we arrived in Fort Myers, I was back at the ballpark playing. What I didn't realize was that instructional league players didn't get paid, which came as a shock to me. I'd been so excited about being invited to play, I'd forgotten to ask about that crucial detail. So I began looking for a part-time job while Lori landed a job as a third-grade teacher at a private Christian school.

That off-season I convinced Lori to let Jason come stay with us for a few months so he could train with me. She was such a good sport. That's when I learned that hanging out with my twin brother as I used to do in college wasn't going to fly in marriage. Jason and I did everything together and didn't think much about it until Lori pulled me aside and told me I should've married my brother. (Jason: I think I'm going to get sick.) That sank in quick. I made a couple of adjustments to my evening schedule, got Jason a job at the lumberyard where I was working for seven dollars an hour, and then did my best to man up as a better husband to Lori. Quick trips with her to Sanibel Island to enjoy the white, sandy beaches and crystal-clear water sure helped things a lot.

That spring, in 1999, the Red Sox invited me to early spring training mini-camp. Only a handful of minor league players attended so they could be pulled up for major league games during spring training, which was another great sign for my career. It was surreal playing with several of the Boston greats, and it was even more surreal when I had the chance to play against one of my childhood heroes, Cal Ripken Jr. I'll never forget watching him take ground balls during batting practice. He donned the Orioles uniform while I stood ten feet away wearing a Red Sox uniform. I was competing on the same field against one of the best baseball players ever to play the game. I could hear *The Natural* music in my ears.

When we broke camp, the Sox sent me to Augusta, Georgia,

to their long season Single-A team in the South Atlantic League, the GreenJackets (like the green jackets the Masters winners wear). After getting hit by a pitch and breaking my left hand, I was sent back to Fort Myers to rehabilitate. By the time I got healthy, I was promoted to the Red Sox's high Single-A team in the Florida State League, the Sarasota Red Sox.

I played well in Sarasota, starting every day and hitting around .300, until a late-season slump dropped me to .240. But everything was still aligning as I continued my ascent toward the big leagues with the Red Sox—until late August when my manager delivered a message I wasn't expecting.

"David, I want to talk to you. Come into my office for a minute."

Eleven

BLUEFIELD BASEBALL

*There may be people that have more talent than you, but
there is no excuse for anyone to work harder than you.*

—Derek Jeter, New York Yankees[1]

While David made his debut in Massachusetts, my Minor
League career began a little farther south. Following a
week of mini-camp after the draft, the Orioles sent me to the
Appalachian League to play for their short season Single-A
team in Bluefield, West Virginia. With a population of only ten
thousand, Bluefield was a perfect baseball town. They treated
minor-leaguers like royalty. On hot summer days, if the tem-
perature rose above ninety degrees, the town gave away free
lemonade on street corners. It felt like a movie set.

Dad always taught us to be valuable wherever God put us by
doing more than we were expected to do, so when I reported to
Bluefield, I prayed for opportunities to do just that. As I prayed,
God put two things on my heart—help the clubhouse attendant

with his job and find an elderly person to visit every week. It reminded me of my early years with David, cleaning the dugouts after Little League games and visiting elderly folks at the nursing home where our mom worked when we were kids.

Helping Out

When I told our clubbie, Morgan, I was going to volunteer as his assistant, he wasn't sure how to respond. You should have seen the look on his face.

I walked up to him and said, "Hey, buddy. Good to meet you. Do you mind if I help you around the clubhouse after games? I can vacuum, wash the uniforms, and polish cleats—whatever you need."

"Are you kidding me? Why in the world would you do that?" he replied.

"Because I'm a Christian, and God told me to help you. Good enough?" I told him.

"Uh, okay. I guess so," he said. "But that's a little odd."

I understood why he didn't get it. It didn't make much sense to me either, but I knew God wanted me to do it. I also knew that making someone else's job a little easier was always a good thing to do. Before I ended the conversation, I asked if he knew of a nursing home nearby I could visit. He then told me about an elderly lady who lived close to the park and was Cal Ripken Jr.'s host mom back in the day when he played in Bluefield. So from that day on, every week when we were in town, I would visit her. It's fascinating how much you can learn from the older generation if you take time to sit with them.

As for helping in the clubhouse, as soon as my teammates left, I'd get to work doing menial jobs, like hanging jerseys in lockers and mopping the bathroom floor. I actually grew to enjoy it—except that the smell of sweat from the jerseys mixed with Lysol pine from the mop stayed in my nostrils for an hour after I left. It's funny because even though I was a late-round pick, which meant I was a small blip on the Orioles' radar, word got around the organization quickly. All the coaches and managers through the system, as well as the players and fans, heard about the Benham kid from Texas who cleaned the clubhouse after the games.

On one occasion my family came to watch me play—Dad, Mom, Abby (who was nine), and Johnny (who was seven). After the game Dad wanted to take us all out to eat, but I couldn't leave until I helped Morgan. We were standing outside the dugout as the last player left, when Dad said to me, "Hey, bud, we could go a lot faster if we all pitch in."

I thought it was a brilliant idea, so I ushered them all into the locker room. Ten minutes later our director of player personnel, Lenny, walked in. The look on his face was worth my entire year's salary (which wasn't much). Mom had the vacuum, Dad was hanging jerseys, Abby and Johnny were picking up trash, and I was putting up laundry bags.

He looked at me, threw his hands up in the air, and shouted, "You have got to be kidding me! Your whole family is just like you—this is crazy!" Then he walked into the manager's office shaking his head.

I looked over at Dad, and he was smiling from ear to ear, as if to say, "See? I told you. When you do more than you're supposed to, it leaves an impression on people."

Lenny

Since I mentioned Lenny, I have to tell you a quick story about him that's vintage minor league baseball. Not only was he the director of player personnel, but he was also our first base coach. One night we were playing against the Texas Rangers' farm team in Pulaski, Virginia, when this drunk dude stumbled out onto the field right next to Lenny at first base. He was only about sixty feet from our dugout, so the whole team watched this unfold.

The guy was shirtless and headed right in Lenny's direction. Now, Lenny was an old guy, around seventy or something. This guy stumbled over to him and looked into our dugout, barking out words we didn't understand and then yelling at the crowd. Suddenly he turned toward the infield, yanked his pants down to his ankles, and mooned the crowd.

Oh yeah, a straight-up full moon was out that night. All the fans, including both teams, burst out in laughter.

But it was short-lived as Lenny, fed up with the guy's disrespect for the game, walked over as he was pulling up his pants and took a swing at him. The dude then cocked his hand back to hit Lenny. I can still see the look on his face just before he swung when he saw our entire team jump off the bench and run right at him.

He took off toward right field, trying to hold his pants up while running away. He made it to the edge of the outfield grass before his pants dropped to his ankles, causing him to fall flat on his face. Our team then dogpiled a buck-naked drunk man. Our pitchers from the outfield bullpen came in hot, which made me fear for the man's safety. So a few of us started pulling the guys off him.

The police eventually stormed the field and got control of the situation. The players on the opposing team were sitting in their dugout doubled over in laughter. The whole fiasco lasted about fifteen minutes and had to be one of the funniest minor league moments of all time.

Only in the Minor League.

Benched?

I played third base for Bluefield most of the season, but about halfway through I found myself on the bench for fifteen straight games. I played well up until that point, so I had no clue what was going on. I wasn't about to approach my manager, Andy Etchebarren, a fifteen-year major league veteran we called "Etch," to ask for an explanation. You just didn't do stuff like that if you valued your position on the team. So I suffered in silence, game after game, bewildered and frustrated.

Eventually I discovered what was happening. The Orioles had another third baseman who was on his last leg with the team, so they were letting him play himself out of a job. They were letting him play for two straight weeks, and if he didn't show them something, I was going to take his spot. Ouch. It just goes to show that we seldom know the full story about what is happening in our lives, but that lots of things are going on behind the scenes. The situation played out exactly as the Orioles expected, and after two weeks the third base job was mine alone.

I had a good season in Bluefield that summer in '98, finishing third on the team in several hitting categories. Late in the year my manager asked me to come see him in his office. In the minor leagues that usually means one of two things: you're getting released, or they're moving you up. He said the Orioles high Single-A team was struggling, and he had suggested to our minor league coordinator that they needed a sparkplug like me.

"You're good for the clubhouse, son," Etch told me. "People like having you around, and I think you're just what those guys up in Frederick need."

This was a big deal for me because it meant I would skip the low Single-A team in Delmarva, Maryland, and head straight up to the high Single-A team in Frederick, a town also in Maryland, just outside of DC.

I left my manager's office totally excited, but as soon as I realized the last game would be on David's wedding day, my heart sank. How do you ask your new manager to skip the last game of the season when you've just been promoted? I put it off until two days before the wedding. I finally mustered the courage to ask him. He just looked at me, as if to say, "Really? You're asking me this?" (David never would have done that for me.)

Fortunately, he said yes, but he wasn't happy about it. I walked out of his office at 10 p.m., hopped in my white Isuzu pickup truck, and drove to the closest Dairy Queen. After crushing the biggest Blizzard I could buy, I drove straight through the night to Torrington, Connecticut, the hometown of my soon-to-be wife, Tori (yes, Tori from Torrington). After spending a little time with her, I drove another four hours north to Portland, Maine, to make the rehearsal dinner. On the way there I got lost and almost missed the dinner. But my late arrival turned out to be one of the most epic rehearsal dinner entrances of all time!

After David's wedding I returned to Torrington to spend the off-season with Tori. While I was there, the Orioles called and invited me to spend three weeks in Lakeland, Florida, playing in the fall instructional league, and, never wanting to pass up a chance to play ball, I said yes right away. Though it was the same league where David was playing for the Sox, we never got to play against each other.

When January 1999 rolled around, I went back to Florida, to stay with David and Lori and get ready for spring training, which became my winter routine every year. It was like old times again, except that I slept on the couch in the living room. We'd get up in the morning, go to the gym, head back to David's for breakfast, then go to the field for a few hours before ending up at the lumberyard to drive forklifts.

In March I reported to Sarasota for spring training and realized that the Red Sox were coming to play us just a few weeks into the season. It would be the first time David and I played against each other in our lives. Up to this point neither of us had told our teammates we had a brother, so none of the players on either team had a clue they were about to see twins.

Before the game, as both teams were stretching in the outfield, I walked over to David and stood next to him. He then called over some of his Dominican buddies, and you would have thought they'd seen a ghost. The words were flying out of their mouths so fast; they kept touching us as if trying to prove to themselves that we were indeed real. They were hysterical with laughter as they danced around us. That was fun. But what was more fun for David was when he hit a bomb against us—a blind dog finds a bone every once in a while.

After spring training I was assigned to the Frederick Keys,

which was a big deal for me. I didn't want to go to low Single A because I was twenty-three and wanted to make significant strides toward the big leagues.

But about fifty games into the season, I began struggling at the plate. My average dropped down around .200 as I lost my confidence and started overthinking again. I felt like I did back at Liberty my first three seasons. It was such a horrible feeling, but this time it was happening as a pro. Unfortunately during slumps like this, it's common for players to fall out of favor with teams—sometimes permanently.

One night I was doing my regular routine of cleaning the clubhouse after a game when Etch, who had moved up from Bluefield to manage at Frederick in 1999, approached me.

"Hey, listen," he said. "We want to teach you to play second base, so we're sending you down."

That wasn't the news I wanted to hear. It hurt. I knew exactly what was happening. Though Etch didn't say much, I could read between the lines—"And if you can't prove you can play second base, your days with the Orioles are over because you're too old." So I packed my bags and headed to Baltimore's low-A team, the Delmarva Shorebirds in Delmarva, Maryland.

Rather than making a good impression by getting off to a hot start, I went the opposite direction. I struggled at second base, a position I'd never played before. A few days later, we headed to Hickory, North Carolina, to play against the White Sox farm team. After the game I ran a few sprints in the outfield, which was my normal routine, and as the lights shut off and the stadium emptied, I spent a few minutes alone in prayer in the outfield.

My heart was heavy at the thought of what was coming if I

didn't start playing better. So right in center field, I got down on my knees and prayed. "Lord, I need something," I said. "Would You please help me? I'm struggling, and I want to play better. My career is Yours, and I pray that You would make something of it. But if You want to take this game from me, then so be it. You gave it to me; You can take it from me. I trust You whatever happens."

The next night, in another game against the Crawdads, God took me up on that offer.

Twelve

MEET ME IN ST. LOUIE

Baseball is 90 percent mental. The other half is physical.

—Yogi Berra[1]

D avid, we just traded you to the St. Louis Cardinals."
That was the message my manager at Sarasota delivered to me when he called me into his office that day late in the 1999 season. The Red Sox were in a pennant race, and one of their star pitchers, Bret Saberhagen, had just gotten hurt. Boston needed to fill his shoes, so they zeroed in on Kent Mercker with the Cardinals, a major league veteran and World Series champion. The Cards asked for two Sox players in return. I was one of those.

"Are you serious?" I said to him. I'd never even entertained the thought of being traded. I knew at some point a trade was possible, but this early in my career it was the last thing I expected. All I could think of was that Lori was in Fort Myers, I was commuting to Sarasota, and things were working out very well for us with only two weeks left in the season.

"The Cardinals want you to fly to Prince William County in Virginia," my manager told me. "You're going to play with the Potomac Cannons in the Carolina League."

In that moment my mind was racing with all kinds of different thoughts as I tried to process the news. Did the Red Sox not want me anymore? What is the Cardinals organization like? What's Lori going to think? Is this good for my career? The questions were unending.

I joined the Potomac Cannons for the last few weeks of the season, hardly enough time to get a feel for the organization before it was over, and I returned home to Florida. I was still trying to make sense of this curveball to my career when the Cardinals invited me to the fall instructional league at their facility in Jupiter, Florida.

Instructs, as we called this fall league, were held at Roger Dean Stadium, the spring training home of the St. Louis Cardinals major league team. When I arrived at the stadium, I ran into Walt Jocketty, the Cardinals' general manager, and John Mozeliak, the scouting director (and later the St. Louis general manager). All the big dogs in the organization were there.

"David Benham, it's nice to finally meet you. You impressed us in Suffolk County, New Jersey, when you were playing with the Lowell Spinners," Jocketty said to me as he introduced himself. "You remember, the night of Chad Hutchinson, right after we signed him?"

Instantly I remembered what he was talking about. Chad Hutchinson had gone to Stanford and was one of the Cardinals' top draft picks in 1998. He held out for most of the summer, negotiating his contract. He finally signed, and the Cardinals sent him to their affiliate in New Jersey. I was playing for the Lowell Spinners at the time, and we were in town the night Hutchinson arrived. News had spread quickly that Chad would be pitching that night.

All the brass from St. Louis came to watch him pitch. I caught that night and hit a few doubles at the plate. It was one of my best games as a pro. Hutchinson only pitched a couple of innings, so we finished the game unloading on their bullpen. We scored something like fifteen runs that night. I even threw out a runner trying to steal second before he started sliding. (Jason: Interestingly enough, my first hit in Frederick was off Chad—a chest-high fastball I should've left alone, but I couldn't help but swing.)

I remember thinking after the game, *Man, that had to be one of the best games I've ever played in my life.* Turns out that performance stood out enough to put me on Jocketty's radar, and when the opportunity came for him to trade Mercker to Boston, he asked for me in return. That conversation clued me in to the fact that the Cardinals were high on me, and they were going to be pushing me through the system.

Walking into the locker room that first day of instructional league, one of the first guys I met was a stocky-looking Dominican. "So I heard they traded for you," he told me.

"Yeah," I said. "You know, I was just a twelfth-round pick. I'm surprised they traded a big-leaguer for me."

"I was a thirteenth-round pick," he told me. His name was Albert Pujols. I had no clue I was talking to a future Hall of Famer. All I knew was that he was a big, humble dude playing fall instructional league with me in the Cardinals farm system. He and I became fast friends.

As I had done with the Red Sox, I started a Bible study with the Cardinals. It became a habit of mine to start a Bible study wherever I was stationed in the minors. In Sarasota with the Red Sox, we averaged about twenty guys every day. We met after batting practice, and I'd go sit on a picnic table outside and share God's Word with my teammates.

For many guys, the Bible studies were a source of hope and encouragement in the middle of their lives of trial and hardship. Lots of people think playing minor league baseball is living the dream, and there's some truth to that. But overall, life in the minor leagues is rough. The system will beat you down if you're not careful because it's a business that's often devoid of hope. I can't imagine going through it without a relationship with God.

After Bible study one day that fall, I was walking around the facility and saw the doors to the big-league locker room were cracked open. Usually those doors were closed, so my curiosity got the best of me, and I decided to have a look.

When I walked in, I was immediately overtaken with the nostalgia of the game of baseball. There before me, hanging above the lockers, were the jerseys of all the Cardinal greats— Bob Gibson, Lou Brock, Stan Musial, Mark McGwire. I was breathless. I dropped to my knees in the middle of the locker room, put my hands up in the air, and prayed. "Lord, in the name of Jesus, get me here." That was all I said because I wanted to get out of there before anyone saw me.

After instructs ended, I spent the rest of the off-season back in Fort Myers with Lori and our infant son, Bailey. Oh, and Jason too. We worked at the lumberyard together again. Something about racing forklifts kept us coming back.

After one of our morning workouts, the last week of January 2000, I got a call from Buddy Bates, the clubhouse manager for the Cardinals.

"David, how do you like your bats?" he asked.

"Uh, y'all make bats for minor-leaguers in St. Louis? The Red Sox never did that."

"Oh, no," Buddy said. "These are major league bats."

"What?"

"No one has told you?" Buddy asked.

"No one has told me what?" I replied.

"Well, you're playing with the major league team for spring training this year," he told me. "So do you want a Louisville Slugger? Rawlings? What kind of contracts do you have in place?"

I had no idea what to tell him. I was speechless. I didn't know I was on the major league spring training team, and I had no clue what kind of bat to make. Fighting back tears of joy, I squeaked out the first thing that came to mind.

"How's McGwire have his bats made?" I asked.

Mark McGwire had just hit sixty-five homers for St. Louis in 1999 after hitting seventy the year before, and that was all I could think of. So I figured I might as well copy him.

"He uses Rawlings, cups the head, with a 243 barrel and a thin handle," he said.

"Great. Make me the same one, only shorter and lighter," I replied.

As soon as I hung up the phone, I plopped down in Lori's glider rocker—the one I bought her to rock our son—and sat in stunned silence. I couldn't believe I was headed to the big leagues to start spring training. It just came out of left field (pardon the pun).

"Thank You, God! All the years, all the prayers, all the hard work—thank You!" I then called Jason with the good news. He knew exactly what this meant—I was now officially on the fast track to the majors. It was a surreal feeling for both of us.

Cardinals Camp

While Jason's minor league spring training with the Orioles didn't start until early March, I had to report to camp for the Cardinals a couple of weeks earlier. I didn't have to twist his arm to convince him to come along with me for my first two weeks of camp.

We showed up on February 15, walking into the big-league clubhouse where I had prayed on the floor a few months earlier. This time the locker room was bustling with activity, and *my* jersey was now hanging in a locker under all the Cardinal greats. Just above my jersey was a placard with the name Benham written in block letters. Above it sat a dozen baseball bats made exactly as I'd specified, with my name burned on the barrel. At the bottom of my locker were enough shoes to start a small shoe store. It felt like a dream. And to top it off, standing in the middle of the room were manager Tony La Russa, Jim Leyland, Bob Gibson, Lou Brock, and Red Schoendienst. All legends of baseball. I couldn't believe it.

La Russa introduced himself to me. Jocketty was there and reminded Tony that the Cardinals had acquired me in the Mercker trade. With all this stuff going on around me, I remembered the scripture, "Do you see a man skilled in his work? He will stand before kings; he will not stand before obscure men" (Proverbs 22:29 NASB). I could see God's hand at work.

I then introduced Jason. Everything in me wanted to ask Jocketty to trade for him, too, but I didn't have the guts to say it. Besides, Jason never would have done it for me, so I was fine with a simple introduction.

As soon as they walked away, the clubhouse manager hustled up to us and introduced himself.

"Hey, David. I'm Buddy Bates—welcome to the big leagues!"

I still couldn't believe my ears.

"Thank you, sir. And thank you for helping me with my bats," I said.

"Oh, it's my pleasure. You know, since this is your first time, why don't you come with me?" he said.

"Do you mind if I bring my brother?" I asked.

"Of course not! Let's go," he replied.

He brought us over to his clubhouse assistant and said, "Hook these guys up."

I didn't really know what he was talking about, but "hooking us up" sounded great to me. He took us to a back room filled with Cardinals gear from wall to wall—every imaginable article of clothing and paraphernalia you can imagine. It was like a Dick's Sporting Goods for Cardinals gear.

"What do you want?" he said.

"Are you serious? I can get whatever I want?" I replied.

"Yep. Whatever you want—take your pick."

At that point Jason finally broke his nervous silence and whispered behind me, "Dude. Get me some shorts and a hat and a—"

"All right, all right," I whispered back.

"Seriously, guys," the clubbie said. "Just have at it."

The two of us walked out of there with arms full of Cardinals gear. Now, remember, we'd grown up on a shoestring budget and were barely scraping by as adults. So this was a moment of absolute luxury for twin brothers from Garland, Texas. We pretty much hooked up every friend and family member we could think of. It's a good thing we arrived so early because no one other than the staff was there to witness our plundering of the clubhouse goodies.

I performed well that spring, but as is typical with most minor-leaguers, I got sent down to the Triple-A team. Just before we broke camp, however, La Russa called me up to play in a big-league game against the Florida Marlins. Halfway through the game he sent me to the plate to pinch hit (take the place of another hitter) against Antonio Alfonseca, this enormous guy with six fingers on each hand.

"David—sit dead red, 95 miles per hour, right down the middle," La Russa told me as I walked to the plate.

I had so much adrenaline pumping through me that I forgot to stretch out and warm up. I just jumped to my feet after sitting for the first four innings, grabbed a bat, smeared on some pine tar, and took a few swings before walking to the plate. I was so pumped I couldn't even feel my legs. "I don't care if he throws it over the backstop," I told myself. "I'm swinging at it."

Alfonseca toed the rubber and looked in for his sign. As La Russa had predicted, he fired a fastball right down the middle. I swung as hard as I could and hammered it right to the third baseman—a worm-burner ground ball. He scooped it up and slung it over to first base, almost before I even got out of the batter's box. As I ran to first, the feeling in my body started to come back again . . . only with a sharp pain in the left side of my ribs.

I returned to the dugout as the guys slapped me with high

fives for the hard hit. But I could barely move my left arm. Then I coughed, and I almost fell over in pain. It felt as though something inside my rib cage had exploded.

Oh no. What did I just do?

Thirteen

BROKEN

*My motto was always to keep swinging. Whether I
was in a slump or feeling badly or having trouble off
the field, the only thing to do was keep swinging.*

—Hank Aaron[1]

Now we need to backtrack a bit to fill in what was happening with me (Jason) the same summer David got traded to the Cardinals. David was on the fast track, as his trade from the Sox to the Cards seemed to open a direct path for him to the big leagues. Of course, I taught him everything, so he has me to thank for his success. He just needed to stay healthy, and he was all set.

My story, however, went a different direction. That summer of 1999 was a real struggle for me. After being sent down to Delmarva, I was desperate for God to do something in my life regarding baseball—to make me better or take it away entirely. Something. Anything was better than the way I was floundering and not making any progress.

While the window to our dream for David seemed to be opening wider and wider, mine seemed to be rapidly closing.

That's why I was so willing to get on my knees in the outfield after the game in Hickory and acknowledge to God that my career was in His hands. It was all along, and I knew that. My prayer didn't mean God took control of something He didn't have control of before. But that acknowledgment was good for me and for my soul. It was a reminder to me that God had all of my days charted out even before I existed, that my baseball career, and my entire life, were His to direct as He saw fit. It's funny how a simple acknowledgment of "God's got this" can bring peace to an anxious heart.

During our game with Hickory the next night, I was playing second base again. The Crawdads had runners on second and third—a perfect opportunity for a squeeze play. The batter squared around for a bunt, with our first baseman and third baseman charging in to make the play. I took off for first base to cover the bag. The bunt went down the third base line. Our third baseman grabbed it, came up, and threw it to me at first.

But there was a problem—the ball tailed away from me into the baseline. Most good first basemen would have let the ball go. I, however, was not a good first baseman. I was not a first baseman at all, nor was I a second baseman. Like an idiot, I dove toward the ball, thinking that I could catch it and make a sweeping tag on the runner to get the out. Doing so, however, left my right leg exposed in midair to the runner. What happened next changed the course of my career as a baseball player.

The runner's knee hit my right leg, snapping my leg in half and shattering my shin. My leg literally wrapped around his. I vividly remember the cracking noise I heard when it happened. If you take a wood bat, hold it by the barrel, and slam the handle down on concrete, that's the kind of breaking sound my leg made. It was bad. Real bad.

I started screaming for my trainer, "PJ! PJ! Help me! I cracked it! I cracked it!" PJ jumped up and came running out of the dugout, along with my manager and coaches. I was lying facedown on my stomach as my body began to go into shock. When PJ grabbed my leg, I heard my manager yell out something I can't put in print. Not what I wanted to hear at that moment. What I didn't realize was that the bone in my shin had popped out of my uniform pants, leaving my leg covered in blood.

"Call the ambulance! Call the ambulance!" PJ yelled.

I continued to lie there for what seemed like forever, with my whole team crowded around me. The guy who had run into me broke his wrist on the play, so he had a group of people around him as well. It must have been quite the sight for the fans. A group of ladies on the front row were bawling their eyes out.

In the distance, I could hear the sound of the ambulance making its way to the stadium. But as I lay there with tears running down my cheeks, I remembered my prayer in the outfield the night before. I had told God He could take the game away if He wanted to. I just didn't think it would happen so fast.

The conversation I had with the Lord as I lay there on that field was so real. In the midst of such a traumatic event, I felt Him close by my side. While the pain in my leg was excruciating, it couldn't match the pain I felt in my heart. I knew it was over and that this is where my dream would die—in an old minor league stadium in the middle of a small North Carolina town.

One by one my teammates came up and patted me on the

shoulder, telling me to hang in there. I could see the pain in their eyes. No player wants to see another player go through that.

The paramedics instantly put an Aircast on me, jabbed a needle into my arm, and started giving me morphine for the pain. Once I arrived at the hospital, they removed my shoe and cut my pants off to work on my leg, then whisked me back for emergency surgery.

I remember praying as they were prepping me for surgery, "Lord, please help me to walk again. If I never play baseball again, that's okay. But I want to be able to play catch with my kids."

It's strange when something that traumatic happens—you begin to think about what's *really* important. The desire to simply walk again was stronger than any other desire I had in that moment.

Meanwhile, I (David) was in Fort Myers, rehabbing from the broken hand I got during the long season with the GreenJackets. I was asleep when the phone rang at about 2 a.m. I saw it was my mom calling.

"Mom?" I said, trying to rouse myself from sleep. "What's going on?"

"It's Jason," she cried, barely able to get the words out through her tears.

"What? Is he dead? What's going on?" The way she was carrying on, I thought something really bad had happened. And, of course, the phone cut out right at that point. I jumped out of bed with my heart pounding out of my chest. "No way! He can't be dead." Lori woke up all freaked-out, wondering what was happening. I tried calling Mom back, but the cell signal was bad.

When I finally reached her, she told me that Jason had broken his leg. "Mom! Don't ever do that to me again! I thought he died," I said. I was so relieved. A broken leg stinks, but I'd already jumped to the worst-case scenario. She was crying so much because she knew his season, and probably his career, was over.

While Jason wasn't dead, one thing I knew for sure—our dream of playing together in Shreveport probably was.

I (Jason) knew going into surgery that my baseball career was finished. The chances of coming back from an injury of this magnitude were slim. My career was already in jeopardy before this accident. Now? In my mind it was time to start thinking about life after baseball.

Fortunately Dad had prepped us for a moment like this. He'd raised us to understand that we are to find our identity in who we are, not what we do. Letting go of baseball wasn't as hard as letting go of the idea of being a professional baseball player. But even though I understood this, it was still a very painful process to go through.

I woke up from surgery with a plaster cast all the way up my leg. My first thought was, *How am I going to go to the bathroom with this bad boy on?*

The doctor came in shortly after. "You snapped your leg," he told me. "It's shattered into pieces. But somehow, some way, when you got in here, all those pieces aligned perfectly back into place, so I didn't have to put a rod in your leg."

Thank You, Lord.

I remember lying there in the hospital room all alone. My mom was on her way to Florida from Texas, but she hadn't arrived yet. I just lay there alone and prayed. And through those conversations, I died to my dream of playing professional baseball.

Thoughts of that prayer in center field a few nights before kept flooding my mind. I couldn't believe God had actually taken me up on my offer. But in spite of how wounded my heart felt, I knew God was doing something. I wasn't sure what it was, and I didn't really like the path He'd chosen, but I was surrendered to walk it with Him.

I knew my career wasn't officially over because professional teams can't release players while they're hurt. So the Orioles had no choice but to let me come back from the injury and play myself out of a job. Still, while nothing was yet official, the death of my dream was real. I knew there was a slim chance it was ever going to happen. Professional baseball of any kind? No way. Shreveport? Not a chance. Playing with my brother? Nope. Lying there on that hospital bed, I resigned myself to figuring out life without baseball.

My mom finally arrived, and after I was released from the hospital, we both went home to Dallas. I spent the rest of that season on the couch in my parents' living room watching baseball on TV. The Red Sox were gracious enough to let David come home to Dallas for three days to visit me after my accident.

Ten months later, following a grueling rehab schedule, I was cleared to play again. But as I was working out with David in Florida before spring training, I could tell I had lost a step. This was the spring David was in big-league camp with the Cardinals, in 2000. I watched him there for a couple of weeks before reporting to my own training camp with Baltimore. The silver lining for me was that I got hooked up with tons of good Cardinals gear. He owed me anyway.

When my spring training ended, I was assigned to start the season in Frederick. I was pretty jazzed up about this because David had been sent to Potomac for rehab, which happened to be in the same league as Frederick. A few weeks into the season, we got to play against each other for a three-game set. Everyone got a good kick out of that—coaches, players, and fans. Since David couldn't play, he threw me soft toss in the cage. If social media had existed then, it would have been a great pic—two opposing players working out with each other before a game.

For me, I was healthy, but I wasn't the same player I had been before. About thirty games into the season, clearly having a hard time of it, I went to the ballpark one day and noticed a bunch of footprints out at second base.

I knew exactly what that meant. They were working someone else out at my position. Although I wasn't surprised, it still hurt to reach that point. I sat on the bench that night. And as the game neared the end, our first base coach yelled and gestured to our manager in the dugout. He pointed at me and then put his fists together, which meant, "Give Benham a chance to hit." He was hoping I wasn't watching, but I saw what was happening. I looked down at our manager, who just shook his head. No at bat for me.

I could feel the tension in the dugout. None of the coaches looked me in the eye. After the game I stayed out on the field signing autographs until everyone was gone. I knew what was coming.

Sure enough, our clubhouse attendant came outside and yelled down to the field, "Hey, Benham. Skipper wants to see you in his office."

Oh boy. God, You've got this.

Fourteen

DYING TO THE DREAM

It's not whether you get knocked down.
It's whether you get up.

—Vince Lombardi[1]

There was something terribly wrong with my side. I (David) could barely breathe in the dugout after my first at bat in big-league spring training. The team doctor took me in for an MRI, and the results confirmed his fears—a tear of the inter-costal muscle, the inner lining of the rib cage. Because I didn't warm up, the muscle wasn't properly stretched out, and the result of my adrenaline rush was a torn muscle that was going to take nearly four months to heal.

So while Jason was making his last-ditch effort to hang on in Frederick after his broken leg, I was now sent back to Potomac for rehab. For the first three months of the season, I couldn't play at all. I couldn't hit. I couldn't catch. I couldn't do anything. Just when my window to the big leagues was opening, it now seemed to slam shut. I knew in spring training that I was on the fast track and was only one phone call away from the majors. At any minute I was going to be there, in the show, living my dream.

Only now, not so much. Compared to Jason's compound fracture, it didn't seem that bad. But still, it was hard. Finally, just before the All-Star break, my rehab was complete and I was activated from the disabled list. My first game for Potomac I went 2-for-3 against the Royals' high-A club. I was back in the game—with a bang.

About ten games later, we were in Salem, Virginia, playing against the Rockies. I had no idea the farm director for the Cardinals—the guy in charge of moving players up or down throughout the system—had called our manager that day to tell him that they were promoting me to Double A and that I'd be flying out to Little Rock the next day.

I was completely clueless that call had taken place. The manager was going to tell me after the game, sharing some of the most exciting news a minor-leaguer can hear: "You're being promoted."

I played that night behind the plate, and late in the game, a hitter fouled a ball off behind the dugout. I ripped off my mask to look for the ball, and the batter recoiled his swing and hit me square in the face with the bat, breaking my nose. It actually shattered my nose in much the same way Jason had shattered his shin.

The manager came rushing out, and his language wasn't pretty.

He stood there shaking his head while our team physician ran on the field with a towel, pushing it against my face to stop the bleeding. He then rushed me to the hospital, where they fixed me up. After the game my manager came to the hospital to pick me up. We rode in silence in the car, with him still shaking his head in disbelief, when his phone rang.

"Hello. Yeah, he's here with me now. Well, I understand . . . there was nothing I could do about it," he said. I could hear a man yelling on the other line—it was our farm director.

"I can't believe you played him tonight! What were you *thinking*?" he shouted.

"I had no idea he was going to break his nose!" my manager told him in defense.

I was still totally in the dark about what was going on. The manager hung up the phone, then turned to me and said, "You were going up to Double A tomorrow morning, but now you're staying with me."

What?! That took my breath away. First, I get hurt in a big-league spring training game and have to sit for several months. Then I break my nose the night before I'm supposed to get promoted to Double A. Talk about hitting the brakes on my dream. It felt like I was watching a golden opportunity walk right past me.

I was honored the Cardinals wanted to move me up to Double A, but I had to stay in Potomac for another month, recovering from yet another injury. It seemed for the first time in my life the deck was stacked against me. I was seriously questioning God about what was going on.

While David was struggling through his 2000 injury-plagued season that slowed his ascent through the Cardinals system, I had an ordeal of my own to deal with. After our clubbie called me away from my autograph session and into the clubhouse, I walked over to our manager's office.

"Hey, Skip, you wanted to see me?"

"Yeah, Tex. Come on in," he responded, shifting in his chair. "Listen, there's no other way to say this, but we've got to let you go."

My chest instantly got hot. Even though I had a hunch this was coming, nothing could have prepared me to hear those words. I felt a lump forming in my throat and tried to fight it back, but as I sat in silence, my lip started to quiver and tears began rolling down my cheeks.

He continued, "I've had to release a lot of guys in my years as a manager, but this is by far the hardest. Everyone knows how hard you've worked to get here, and everyone in the organization loves you. But we have to move on."

He then got up from his desk and hugged me.

There's nothing like the feeling of giving it your all, only to hear someone say you're not good enough. That was hard. I felt broken. I knew when I'd injured my leg that this day might come, but it didn't soften the blow when it finally did.

As I walked out of his office, there was a hushed silence in the clubhouse. Players have a sixth sense for when someone is getting released. Nobody knows when it's going to happen, but when it does, there's a somber quiet that falls over the clubhouse. I wasn't alone that night, as another player on the team had also been cut.

I sat down at my locker and put my head in my hands, tears hitting the floor. I tried to stop, but I couldn't. Thoughts of what the game of baseball meant to me for so many years flooded my mind—playing catch in the backyard with Dad, listening to Mom ring her cowbell, driving past Shreveport with David, hearing Grampa scream, "Fire it in there!"

Getting released wasn't just the death of *my* dream; it was the death of *our* dream. My whole family was part of this. I'd wanted to play professionally and make it to Shreveport for them just as much as I wanted to for myself. But now it was over.

As I sat there, a teammate of mine came over to console me. Although he was the polar opposite of me in every way, we'd become good friends throughout our years with the O's.

As I wrote in our book *Living Among Lions*, he was a consummate ladies' man and prided himself in how good he looked and smelled, at all times. He would even shower between batting practice and game time and then spray his whole body with cologne. While we were on the field stretching, we could smell him the moment he stepped out of the clubhouse. All the guys joked he was the best-smelling dude on the team. He seemed to relish his reputation as he rolled onto the field with a big smile and an even bigger swagger in his step.

But on this night his swagger was gone. As I sat there with my head in my hands, I felt a tap on my shoulder. When I looked up, there he was. He pulled me up and hugged me as tight as he could. Then he reached out and handed me a gift he said was especially for me. I looked, and there was his trademark bottle of cologne.

I could tell he was having a hard time processing my release. From his perspective, it flew in the face of the traditional thinking that "bad things shouldn't happen to good people." With all seriousness, he looked right at me and said, "You're the real deal, man. I love you and don't want you to ever forget me. When you smell my cologne, think of me, and pray for me."

I still have it today.

I walked out of the clubhouse that night for the last time as a professional baseball player. The thought hit me, *Man, if only I could have played with David in Shreveport—to have gotten just one at bat in that stadium and fulfilled our lifelong dream together.* But that wasn't going to happen.

Before I left the stadium, I stopped at a pay phone beside one of the concession stands. The stadium was dark by this time, so I was able to be alone. I called Tori. I called David. I called my parents. It hurt each of them just as much as it did me.

Dad, in typical fashion, said, "Well, Jeets, praise Jesus! You've been faithful to Him. Now, let's just see what He has in store for you." It was a well-timed reminder that God always knows what He's doing, and He's working behind the scenes even when we can't see Him.

When I got back to my host family's house, they were still up in spite of the late hour. Their son was our batboy, so he had given them the news already. Without mincing words, they asked if I could get one of our first-round picks to take my place and live with them. I had just been released, my lifelong dream was over, and my host family was more interested in housing my replacement than in me. It was funny and sad all at the same time.

The next day I left Frederick to drive to Torrington, Connecticut, where Tori was living. The Torrington Twisters, where I had played that summer during college, were just about to begin their season. I hoped I could spend the summer coaching them and hanging out with Tori while I tried to decide what to do with the rest of my life. Coach Mo wasn't coaching there anymore, so they hired me as their hitting coach for the summer.

A few days later I had to go back to Frederick to pick up a few things and tie up some loose ends. I drove by the stadium that night. The lights were on, my old team was playing, and I was driving by, just like a normal Joe. It was the first time I felt that I was now a regular person. I was not a baseball player. If I were to walk into that stadium, I'd have to buy a ticket and sit in the stands just like everybody else. One night everyone wanted my autograph; the next night nobody cared. It was a humbling moment.

I spent the rest of the summer as a hitting coach in Torrington. I have to be honest—I dreaded every minute of it. Aside from getting engaged to Tori that summer, which was the highlight of my time there, I was miserable. I didn't want to be a coach—I wanted to be a player. And coaching every day was a consistent reminder that I wasn't good enough to play.

I remember sitting in the dugout one game when our manager walked in with several boxes of Snickers ice cream bars. As a player, I wouldn't have touched them, especially during a game. But now that I was a coach, I went all in and ate an entire box. That was my low point. (David: Uh, I think it could have actually been a high point—Snickers ice cream bars are amazing.)

But gradually, day by day, God brought me through. It wasn't like flipping a switch. Instead, a little bit at a time, I began to let go of my dream. By God's grace, I never stopped reading my Bible or spending time with the Lord. I wasn't mad at God for taking the game from me. Dad had taught us better than that. He would say, "If you only love God for what He gives you, then you'll hate Him for what He takes from you."

I didn't know what I was going to do when the summer ended, or what I was going to do for years to come without baseball. But I knew deep down that I'd be okay and God would work everything out as He saw fit.

By the end of the summer, I had fully embraced the fact that my baseball playing days were over. While I wasn't exactly happy about it, I had made my peace with it. It would have been nice to play longer, and it would have been mind-blowing to play in Shreveport, even if just once. But that wasn't going to happen. So I decided to focus my energies on something more productive. I had to figure out what I was going to do with my life, and dwelling on what might have been didn't help me move forward.

Just as our season was about to wrap up in Torrington, I got a call from David in Little Rock, Arkansas, where he had been promoted to Double A.

"Hey, man! You should come visit me for the last few weeks of the season."

A SUMMER VISIT

There are some people who live in a dream world,
and there are some who face reality; and then
there are those who turn one into the other.

—Douglas H. Everett[1]

After recovering from my broken nose, I (David) had finally been promoted to the Cardinals' Double-A team in Little Rock—the Arkansas Travelers—shortly after the All-Star break in 2000. The Travelers played in this great old ballpark, Ray Winder Field, which opened back in the 1930s.

If only that stadium could talk—the games it's seen and the stories it could tell. Dad raised us to truly appreciate the nostalgia of the game, so I was not going to let the opportunity to soak it in pass me by. It reminded me of the old stadiums I saw in *The Natural*. Just hearing the crack of the bat and the sound of balls ricocheting off the tin roof of the grandstand was enough to make you feel as though you were playing back in the '30s.

Though I hadn't been in Arkansas long, I was having a good year, playing almost every day. It was unbelievably hot there. It reminded me of mini-camp back with the Red Sox, only I didn't have the luxury of retreating to the ocean after the game. We were smack-dab in the middle of Little Rock, melting at Ray Winder Field all summer long. Lori was with me for a while, but as the end of the season neared, we decided that she'd go back home to Fort Myers with our one-year-old son, Bailey. At least she was going to get some beach time before the summer ended.

Meanwhile, Jason's season in Torrington had ended, and he began making plans to go back to Liberty to take a few classes for his master's degree. Knowing he had several weeks before he had to report to class, I got the idea he should come and spend the last two weeks of the season with me.

"Dude, I know you've got nothing to do for the next few weeks," I told him. "Come and hang out with me in Little Rock. We'll work out in the mornings, and then you can come with me to the games at night."

I thought this was a no-brainer. So what was with the dead air on the other end of the line?

I (Jason) had just spent an entire summer getting over the game of baseball, so I was hesitant to agree to David's plan. I knew being around David in the minors would stir up all those emotions again. I had made peace with the fact that my playing days were over, so I didn't want to eat, breathe, and sleep baseball again. I was ready to distance myself from the game and move on with my life.

But David kept pressing. I figured it was because he was

scared to be by himself after Lori went back to Florida, so he needed me to come and sleep in the same room as him, like we did back in the day. I finally agreed to do it—but not because he begged. I agreed because my fiancée, Tori, had never been to my hometown of Dallas, and we'd already planned to go there and spend some time together before I headed back to Liberty. If I drove to Arkansas, spent a week or so with David, then headed down to Dallas, I'd save the money on a plane ticket.

So I packed up my truck and took off from Torrington in late August and headed southwest toward Little Rock. The game that night had already started when I got to town. I remember pulling up to the park, getting out of my truck, and seeing the lights of the stadium. I could hear the bat hitting the ball and the ball popping in the glove as the fans cheered loudly. I had never stepped foot in a Double-A stadium before. It was quite a bit bigger than any place I had played in Single A.

The minute I walked inside, I was overwhelmed with that old, familiar minor league-park smell—the freshly mown grass, the pine tar and well-worn leather, off-the-grill ballpark hot dogs, fresh popcorn, and even the peanuts. All of it came rushing back. *I've been here before*, I thought to myself. *Just not in this situation.*

Everything was so familiar but so brand new. I was accustomed to watching games from the dugout, but now I had to watch from the stands. Being a coach meant I still wore a uniform and at least was allowed on the field, but now the only way I could get into a game was with a ticket, and my only seat was with the fans. I remembered the feeling I had of being an average Joe the night I went back to Frederick and passed by the stadium. But on this night I had to walk inside and watch the game. The thought of being a spectator while my brother was still a player sank deep inside my heart.

As I made my way through the stadium, it wasn't easy for me. Being in Torrington gave me a unique distance from the game. Yes, it was still baseball, but it wasn't *professional* baseball. Those college players weren't living my dream—these professional players were. But during those months of coaching, I had truly died to the game of baseball. I felt the Lord giving me peace that His will was better than mine and I could trust Him to direct my steps.

But walking through the stadium that night, I began to feel that old pull inside me—that yearning to play the game that had been such a big part of my life for as long as I could remember. *Man! I wish I could have at least made it to Double A. That would have been amazing,* I thought. *To play in a park this big and face competition this good would have been like making it to the big leagues.*

I (David) was sitting on the bench that night, so I was in the bullpen along the right field bleachers. We were playing the Wichita Wranglers (a Texas Rangers farm team), and I had left a ticket for Jason at the gate. I remember looking up and seeing him strolling down the bleachers toward me, wearing a T-shirt, shorts, and flip-flops. It felt so weird to be in a uniform with Jason sitting in the stands. This was a first for both of us.

He plopped down in the front row, right behind where I was sitting in the bullpen. A few of our pitchers didn't know I was a twin, so when they saw Jason, they were pretty freaked-out. That was the best part of being separated—we got to pull a lot of pranks on people who had no clue we were twins.

We talked the whole game. We hadn't seen each other all summer and had a lot to catch up on. I was actually glad I was on the bench that night.

"So what's it like being a coach?" I asked.

"Boring. I just wanted to grab a bat and say, 'Here's how it's done, boys!' But, instead, I had to sit in the dugout and simply watch things happen on the field," Jason replied.

"It's going to be weird going back to Liberty and not be on the baseball team," I added.

"Yeah, don't remind me. It's hard enough already," Jason replied.

After the game we went back to my host family's house. They were thrilled Jason was coming to stay with me. But Jason wasn't too excited when he realized the only place for him to sleep was the other side of my full bed with me. We'd slept in the same bed so many times in our lives when traveling, we just picked up right where we left off—we built our customary "force field" of pillows in between and hopped in.

Just before we dozed off, I asked him, "So what's it really like? What's life like without being a baseball player?"

"Dude," Jason replied, "it's been hard. But time has helped me. There's actually a part of me now that's glad it's over. I started to feel the urge to play again tonight when I walked into the stadium, but I was able to push it back. I'm finally to a point where I can move on with my life."

He told me about the episode with the entire box of Snickers ice cream bars. I laughed out loud when he explained the reason why. He said, "I looked down at that box and heard those sweet little rectangular slices of heaven tell me, 'Nobody knows you and nobody cares, so just eat us right up, you big stud!'"

I could see myself doing the same thing. Ice cream just makes everything feel better.

Before dozing off, I outlined our plan for the following day. "Tomorrow we'll go to the field early and take some batting practice," I told him.

"Nope! Not gonna do it," Jason kicked back.

Sometimes I just like telling David no. It's good for him to hear. Actually, this time I was afraid that stepping on the field and taking some swings might stoke the fire and make me want to get back into baseball. I was finally at a place where I was at peace, and I was content with not playing. Doing something like that was risky because I knew it could undo everything I'd accomplished over the past several weeks in moving past the game.

"Dude, relax. You don't have to hit; just throw me some balls. I need the work," David said.

I lay there in bed with a whirlwind of emotions. I wanted to help David make it to the big leagues, but I didn't want to stir up the desire to play again. But David was pushy, and—like always—he wasn't going to leave me alone until he got his way.

"All right, I'll go," I finally said, "but you better not ask me to hit."

"Good! Now quit talking and let me get some sleep," David said, just before we zonked out for the night. "We'll head out to the field early—it's going to be like old times."

Sixteen

HOME RUN DERBY

*Somebody once asked me if I ever went up to the plate
trying to hit a home run. I said, "Sure, every time."*

—Mickey Mantle[1]

The next morning we got up and hit our customary routine—
Bible reading, workout, monstrous breakfast, then off to the
ballpark for a long-overdue session of batting practice together.
When we got into the clubhouse, David walked over and put his
workout gear on while I looked around at all the lockers with
the uniforms hanging in them, remembering when I'd hung
uniforms in Bluefield and Frederick. While it may sound odd,
I missed hanging those things up. Mostly, I think, it's because
hanging them up meant I would also get to put one on.

After he got dressed, we walked through the tunnel together
into the dugout and then onto the field. By this time George
Strait was playing over the public address system, bringing us
back to those hot summer days when we played in high school.

The batting cage was already set up, along with a big five-gallon sunflower seed bucket filled with baseballs, so we walked over to get to work.

Nobody else was out there. It was just the two of us. We warmed up a little bit, and then I started throwing batting practice (BP) to him. Throwing good BP is an art, and I was its maestro. David would be the first to tell you that I was his favorite BP pitcher.

David said he had some weak areas to work on at the plate. So he hit some to the opposite field, a few up the middle, and then started working the whole field. Before long, the outfield was filled with balls. When the bucket was empty, he put the bat down, and the two of us trudged out to right field to pick up the balls. By the time we got to center field, poor David couldn't resist the urge any longer.

"Dude, why don't you just take a few swings?" he asked.

"No way," I said. "You told me you wouldn't ask."

But he persisted. "Come on, man! What's it going to hurt? You haven't even swung a bat the whole summer. Just hit a few pitches. You'll love it."

I continued to reject the idea. David continued to press it.

"I've got some really good big-league wood," he said. "The kind with the wide seams. You'll love the feel of the ball off these bats. You have to try it."

I could see Jason looking down at the stack of bats lying on the ground. I was slowly breaking him down to get what I wanted, an art I had perfected over twenty-five years as his twin.

He looked up at the field and then looked back down at the

bats. He did this a few times before finally saying, "Okay—but just a *few* swings."

Job well done on my part, I must admit.

He wasn't ready to hit at all. He was wearing flip-flops and shorts—perfect gear for watching the game but not so good for playing it. As I walked out to the mound to get loose, he grabbed one of my bats and started warming up. This felt like the old days—I hit while he pitched; then he hit while I pitched.

Jason stepped into the box, dug in, and waited with hands held high. Ever since Coach Mo taught him the bat cock, he had held his hands quite a bit higher than I did. I grabbed a ball and tossed it toward the plate.

Whack!

The first pitch he'd seen in three months—launched over the right field wall onto I-35. *Okay. He got lucky*, I thought. Until I threw him the next pitch.

Whack!

Another bomb over the right field wall. It got a bit more interesting. Another pitch.

Whack!

This one went even farther than the other two and bounced on the highway. I couldn't believe what I was seeing. I just kept pitching.

One after another, hard line drive, home run, hard line drive, home run. Opposite field. Dead center. Right field. Pitch after pitch after pitch. He was absolutely killing it, lighting up the field and sending balls all over the place. He was actually hitting better than me, which was hard for me to believe, of course. A few years earlier I had witnessed his epic turnaround our senior year at Liberty, but his swing now was on a whole different level.

We got through about half the bucket of balls before he nearly fell over from exhaustion. I got a good laugh out of that. When you haven't swung a bat in a long time, and then you get in and start hacking, it's hard work. He was totally gassed and dripping with sweat.

"Get up, dude. We've got to pick up all these balls," I said.

So we headed to the outfield with our half-filled sunflower seed bucket of balls. By the time Jason got his breath back, he looked over at me and said, "I told you I shouldn't have done that. I can feel it coming back."

I (Jason) knew something like that could happen if I cracked open the door. I knew that part of dying to a dream meant you had to stay away from it lest it come back to life in the early stages. When I felt that bat in my hands and watched that ball sailing over the wall, I started to feel an intense pull to play again. Baseball was too much a part of me to expect that I had purged myself of its pull after only a few months. I had devoted much of my life to the game. It's what I breathed. It was the foundation for many of the relationships in my life. It had been my dream all my life. And David had set me up to feel this all over again!

Even if I had not taken BP that day in Little Rock, I'm sure something else would have triggered my desire eventually. Whatever the reason, God allowed it to happen on that day, with my brother and my flip-flops, at that old Arkansas stadium. The rush I felt after hammering ball after ball into the gap, over the fence, and off the wall came surging back with a vengeance. It's kind of like what David feels after a spoonful of ice cream.

By the time we picked up the last ball, I felt a burning like I hadn't felt before. It wasn't just the desire to *play* but a desire to *pray*. It was an insatiable feeling to pray and ask God for something miraculous. Something only He could do. I felt a holy boldness come over me as if God Himself were whispering in my ear, *Talk to Me. Whatever's in your heart, just ask Me. I can do miracles.*

I looked over at David, feeling a lump in my throat as my heart began pounding faster and faster. The weight of God's presence was so powerful in that moment; I had a hard time containing my emotions. David could tell I was having a moment, and I think he knew what I was about to ask.

"Dude, let's pray," I said. "Let's ask God to let me play again. And not just play again but play on this team, with you, for the rest of this season."

David looked back at me as if I had three eyes. "Are you serious?" he said, shaking his head in disbelief. I knew the probability of David's team—or any team—signing a washed-up free agent who never played above Single A and hadn't laced up the cleats in months was slim to none. But it just blurted out of my mouth. I felt such strong faith in that moment, and I knew that if David and I prayed, God would hear us. I wasn't sure what it would all look like, but I had to ask.

Jason had that look in his eyes. I initially felt the weight of improbability like an anchor pulling me into the deep. I had already seen Jason go through so much heartache in the game of baseball—I didn't want to see him have his heart broken again. But I could feel the spiritual excitement coming from him. He was beaming and smiling from ear to ear.

"God can do this," he said. "He's already proven He can do the impossible by getting us full-ride scholarships to Liberty, changing my swing in Torrington, getting us both drafted. Remember when He orchestrated my hit-and-run home run at George Mason? He's the God of miracles. Why not trust Him for a massive one, an impossible one, again?"

In much the same way that I was shocked at the turnaround in his swing, I could see the same was happening with his faith. And it was contagious. I wanted to believe like that, and the more Jason pressed, the more I realized what I already knew to be true—God can do whatever He wants whenever He wants with whomever He wants however He wants. He didn't have to ask me anymore—I was ready to ask God to do the impossible.

"All right. Let's do it," I said.

So, as we'd done many times on high school and college baseball fields across Texas and the Southeast, we got down on our knees in center field, bowed our heads, and poured out our hearts to the Lord.

"Lord Jesus, please," Jason prayed, "please let me play again. You know my heart has already let the game go, but for some reason I feel like it's not over for me yet. I want to play, with David, here in Little Rock, for the Cardinals. I have no idea how You're going to do it, but I know You can, and You will if it's Your will. Please, God, just one more chance."

Then I prayed, "Lord, I ask in Jesus' name that You would do this for us. Please let Jason sign with the Cardinals and play here. We don't know how, but we trust You."

By the time we were done, our hearts were filled with child-like faith, right there in center field, as we begged God for a miracle.

We got up quickly, hoping no one had seen us. Yet we had a spiritual fervency that felt electric. The excitement of pouring our hearts out to God and waiting expectantly for His answer drew us into His presence in a very real way. We felt confident that we could trust Him, and that however He decided to handle this request, we would be okay with it.

We walked back into the clubhouse, and David got dressed for the game. The other players were arriving, so I walked back and took my average Joe seat in the stands to watch the teams warm up. I just sat there by myself, trying to control the anxious thoughts that typically come when you make a bold prayer request as we had just done. Before BP I'd had peace and contentment in my heart that the game was over for me. But now the dream had come alive again. I continued to pray, asking God to give me grace to accept His will, whatever that might be.

Just before game time David walked over and told me he was in the bullpen again that night, so I headed down the right field line to hang out with him on the front row during the game.

Then, in the seventh inning, something very interesting happened.

Seventeen

A CRAZY IDEA

I swing with everything I've got. I hit big or I miss big.

—Babe Ruth[1]

It happens multiple times in a game: a player slides into the base—a routine play that occurs dozens of times a week and hundreds of times a year for a team, almost always without incident.

On this night, however, things were not so routine. Our team was up to bat and our second baseman, Alex, was on first. With the steal sign on, he took off toward second base and slid in for a bang-bang play. The ball beat him to the bag—he was out. But when he emerged from the cloud of dust, we could see him hobbling back to the dugout holding his wrist.

We didn't think anything of it at the time—players get thrown out every day—it's not a big deal. But when Alex didn't come out of the dugout for the next inning, we knew something was up.

I (David) made a quick trip from the bullpen to the dugout to get the lowdown, only to find out from our trainer that Alex had sprained his wrist. Although the injury wasn't serious, he would most likely have to sit out the remainder of the season.

Nobody likes to see a teammate hurt. Even so, the first thought that went through my mind was, *Wait a minute; Jason plays second.* I felt a small glimmer of hope.

By the time I made it back down to the bullpen, I could tell the wheels inside Jason's head were spinning. But they started whirling even faster when I told him it looked like Alex might have to sit out for the final week of the season. I knew what he was thinking—this could be the open door we prayed about.

We both knew a lot of dominoes had to fall to replace a guy in Double A. Putting a player on the disabled list (DL) was just the first step. Then a replacement for him had to be called up from a lower level. That begins the trickle-down effect, when you have to replace that player, and then that player, and so on. It's a lot of moving parts, a ton of paperwork, and a boatload of headache for the farm director. And with fewer than ten games left in the season, it could potentially be an opportunity for Jason. But I didn't let myself go there. Yet.

The next day it was confirmed—Alex was out for the remainder of the year. From the outside, you would think this was an unfortunate event, but for Alex, as well as most other minor-leaguers, the opportunity to skip the last few games of a grueling season because of a minor injury is actually a relief.

It was hard to see a player get hurt out there. Still, I remembered the prayer we had prayed earlier that day in the outfield, and I felt as though God had just pushed the first domino. I didn't want to get too excited because there was still much more for the Lord to do to bring about our miracle, but for the first time in a long time, Jason had a glimmer of hope.

I have to admit, the thought of him even having a possibility to play again felt good. While we weren't happy about Alex's injury, we also knew it wasn't serious and he'd be back in full swing next year.

That night, as we lay there in bed separated by our pillow force field, I said to Jason, "Dude, it's really crazy what happened today."

Before I finished my sentence, Jason responded, "Man, I'm telling you, God is doing something. And I think I know what the next move is."

"What?" I questioned.

"I've thought this all through," he said, like a mad scientist concocting a secret formula. "We both know the Cards have to bring up a player from Single A to take his place, but he will most likely just be a backup. That will start the domino effect of moving players at each level. And do you think they want to do all that in the last week and a half of the season? Not a chance. We can save them the headache."

Itching to give me the specifics of his plan, he continued, "Tomorrow, you need to talk to your manager, Hammer. [We had crazy names for all our managers.] Tell him your brother played second base in the Orioles organization. Tell him to call your minor league director and pitch him the idea of signing me to fill in for Alex so they don't have to go through all the hassle of moving players around. They don't even have to pay me—I'll play for free."

I lay there in silence. He had thought this all through, and it made sense. I was actually surprised I hadn't thought of it before him since I'm so much smarter. But I wasn't exactly sure I wanted to stick my neck out for Jason like that since I was trying to establish myself as a key prospect for the Cardinals. I was only a phone call away from the big leagues, and I didn't want to come across to the organization as if I was begging them to let my little brother play with me. It was win-win for Jason, but for me, if this plan went south, I was the one who would pay the price for it.

It was a risk for something that honestly had no chance of happening anyway, apart from a miracle. But there was something inside my heart that felt the same way Jason did. Although it was a bit scary for me, it was also exhilarating to think that maybe, just maybe, God could open the hearts of the decision makers in the Cardinals system to give Jason a shot to play again—with me—just as we'd prayed.

"Dude, this is exactly what we prayed for," Jason continued. "How can we be sure this isn't God's way of answering our prayer unless we move on to the next step?"

Even though I lay there without saying a word, the whole time I was talking to the Lord. *Is this part of the answer to our prayer, God? Do You really want me to talk to my manager tomorrow?*

The next day I was at the field for batting practice while Jason sat in the stands and watched. When it was my group's turn to hit, I trotted in from the outfield and headed over to get my bat. As I stood there putting pine tar on the handle, Jason made his way down to the front row.

"Dude, go talk to Hammer. This is our one shot. They're probably making plans to replace Alex right now, so you need to do this today," he said.

My heart sank. Not because I didn't want to do it but because I feared the repercussions if things didn't work out. I had no clue how Hammer would respond to a ridiculous request like this. It was so off the wall and definitely outside the box of normal player and manager conversations.

But I realized that if the roles were reversed, Jason would do it for me (maybe). So I took a deep breath, said a quick prayer, gritted my teeth, and made my way over to Hammer, who was standing behind the cage with a piece of straw in his mouth (every manager has his interesting habits). His hat was cocked back as he leaned against the cage watching the players hit. My heart was pounding as I approached him.

Trying to be as discreet as possible so the other players wouldn't hear me, I whispered, "Hey, Hammer. Um, I know you guys put Alex on the DL yesterday, and that means you'll have to move some players around to fill his spot. That's a lot of shuffling the deck for just a few games. I have an idea that would save the Cards money, time, and headache."

Hammer just stood there, chewing on his straw, only looking in my direction for a split second before turning back to the hitter. I knew at this point I had officially jumped into the deep end with both feet, so I just went for it.

"I think we should sign my brother. He played infield for the Orioles but was released a few months ago. He's here with me now and could fill Alex's spot. If we signed him, we wouldn't have to deal with the headache of shuffling around all those other players, and it will also save the Cards money because he would play for free."

No response from Hammer—nothing but crickets. I ended, saying, "Just have Jorgy [our farm director, Jorgenson] pull a scouting report on him, and he'll see he can play the game. Signing my brother would make his job a lot easier."

Hammer didn't flinch. He barely said a word. The conversation was over.

I felt like an idiot. For one brief moment on behalf of my brother, I became *that* guy: "Hey, Coach, will you sign my little brother?!" What a moron.

I watched as David talked to Hammer. I was praying the entire time. I asked God to open Hammer's heart in the same way He had done so many times in Scripture with others. I was literally standing on the promises of God—that He could change men's hearts if He wanted.

But it seemed Hammer wasn't even listening. He looked like a brick wall. It was hard not to let doubt creep in.

When batting practice was over, I walked over to where Jason was standing. I could tell he was eager to see how my conversation with Hammer went. "Dude, don't get your hopes up. I have no clue what he's thinking. He barely even acknowledged me," I said.

We played that night, but no word. The next day at BP, I wanted so bad to ask Hammer what he thought of my suggestion, but I resisted the urge. I figured I'd already done enough damage to my reputation and maybe even to my future with the team.

After the game that night, having heard nothing from Hammer, we both felt pretty discouraged. "I don't think they liked our plan," I told Jason.

"Yeah, me neither," he replied. "But it was fun to take a swing."

I (Jason) remember vividly what I felt that night. I had prayed in faith, trusted in faith, and even saw things starting to turn my way. But when it appeared it wasn't going to work out, I felt strangely content. Although I was a bit discouraged by the fading prospect of playing again with David, I was energized by the fact that we had taken a shot. David and I trusted God together to do something miraculous, and even if it didn't work out the way we wanted, I knew God was pleased with our faith.

It was an odd feeling, to be honest. But it brought to life a passage from Philippians that says, "Do not be anxious about anything, but in every situation, by prayer and petition, with thanksgiving, present your requests to God" (4:6). David and I both had done this part—we had made our request with thankful hearts to the Lord. But now, with the thought of our request being denied, I began to experience the second part of that passage: "And the peace of God, which surpasses all understanding, will guard your hearts and minds in Christ Jesus" (4:7 csb).

It didn't make sense at all, but I felt peace—true peace. The kind that surpasses understanding. I knew that no matter what happened, God was in control—and He could be trusted. I was thankful for that.

The next day we went to a park in the neighborhood where David lived and, unfortunately for him, I proceeded to spank him in a game of one-on-one basketball, like I used to do when we were kids. After hoops, we hit a body-weight workout on the playground, using the monkey bars for pull-ups and platforms for push-ups, and then headed back to the house to crush some lunch before going to the ballpark.

Just about the time we finished lunch, the phone in the kitchen rang.

A NEW DAY

Today I consider myself the luckiest
man on the face of the earth.

—Lou Gehrig[1]

Hello?" I (David) said as I picked up the wall-mounted, landline phone (the old-school type, with no caller ID and a long spiral cord attached).

"Hey, David, this is Aaron," our clubhouse manager said on the other line. "I've got a quick question for you. Is your brother Jason still in town?"

"Yeah," I replied.

"Good," he said. "Because Jorgy just called Hammer and said the Cards want to sign him."

I was stunned, literally. I could barely feel my arm holding the phone as his words echoed in my ear.

"Are . . . are you serious?" I asked, still thinking this could possibly be some kind of cruel joke. But since I hadn't told any of the guys on the team about my conversation with Hammer a few days before, I thought maybe he was actually serious.

"Yep," he responded. "Bring him to the field. I've got his contract right here."

I hung up the phone, and the numbness I felt in my arm began to go through my whole body. *Are you* kidding *me?* I thought to myself as I stood there in shock. *This is a miracle—like Jesus raising someone from the dead or something.* I turned quickly to find Jason.

As soon as I turned around, he was standing right behind me, smiling from ear to ear.

"They want to sign me, don't they?" he asked, nodding his head up and down.

"I . . . I can't believe it," I replied in disbelief. "That was the clubbie. He just told me they want to sign you for the rest of the season."

Honestly, I can't remember exactly what we did next. In Jason's world we probably hugged, while he laid his head on my shoulder and scream-cried or something, but not in my world. All I recall is the two of us standing together, just shaking our heads in total amazement.

We were witnessing firsthand the miraculous reality of Proverbs 21:1: "The king's heart is like channels of water in the hand of the LORD; He turns it wherever He wishes" (NASB). God had divinely turned the hearts of the Cardinals' leadership our direction as they offered Jason a contract to play at the Double-A level with me. It was an awesome feeling.

How in the world did God pull this off? I wondered.

"Dude, this has got to be the most amazing thing I've ever seen in my life," I said, breaking the silence. "I can't believe it!"

"I'm overwhelmed," Jason replied as he hit his knees. "Let's pray and thank the Lord."

We both got down on our knees right there by the phone in the kitchen, raising our hands toward heaven just as we had in the outfield two days before, and we thanked God for His divine hand of intervention in our lives.

"God, why are You so good to me?" Jason prayed. "Thank You so much. I don't deserve this, but I'll take it! Thank You, thank You, thank You. You are more faithful than I ever could have imagined."

I (Jason) specifically remember the feeling of confidence that came over me while David was on the phone, and I heard him say, "Are you serious?" It wasn't confidence in myself but confidence in God—I knew in my heart the Lord was about to do something spectacular. When David said those words, I felt a rush of adrenaline flood my body—every hair stood on end as I clung to the hope that it was someone from the Cardinals on the other line. From the expression on David's face, I could tell he was having a hard time finding words to say (that's not normal for him), which to me meant something good was about to happen.

It's hard to describe a moment like this. My whole life I'd had a dream, but then I had to die to it after breaking my leg— only to get the dream back again with a full recovery the next season, only to have to die to it all over again the day I was released by the Orioles.

Now, I was in Little Rock, Arkansas, watching my brother play Double-A ball with the Cardinals—and God totally resurrected my dream from the dead. The story of Mary and Martha, when Jesus raised their brother, Lazarus, from the dead became so real to me (John 11:1–44). I felt as if God had just rolled back the stone and pulled my dream of playing professional baseball together with David out of the grave!

We didn't waste any time getting to the ballpark that afternoon. The very first thing I did was find a pay phone to call my parents. (We didn't have cell phones yet.) When Dad answered, I said, "Dad, are you sitting down?"

"No," he replied. "But I can. Why?"

"Because I just signed to play with the Cardinals. I'm on David's team in Double A!"

"You're kidding me!" he replied in disbelief.

"No. It's for real. But I can't talk right now because I have to go into the clubhouse and sign the contract."

"Mom, you're not going to believe this," Dad yelled across the house to tell her the good news. "Jase is going to play with David on the Travelers!"

I had to hold the phone away from my ear as she screamed. I figured I'd hear something like that from her. I'm just glad she didn't ring her cowbell.

"Buddy," Dad said before hanging up, "you have to see God doing all of this. He has His hand on you and your brother, and He's giving you both a testimony of His mighty power. The same God who parted the Red Sea is working for you, making a way when it seems there is no way. Never forget this. Take it all in—don't miss any of it."

I hung up the phone and quickly ran down to the clubhouse, where David was waiting for me before going in. We wanted to do this together. As soon as we walked in, I saw my locker.

There was my jersey, hanging with my name on the back and a placard over the top that read, "J. Benham." Just a few feet away was David's locker. We hadn't seen that since college. The club-house manager walked up to me with the contract in his hand. "Hey, Jason. Sign here, here, and here. Welcome to the team!"

I never even looked at what I was signing, nor did I care. I was on the team, and that was good enough.

In all my excitement, I didn't realize I had no baseball gear with me at all. I had to borrow everything—a glove, cleats, batting gloves, a bat, and one dude was even kind enough to lend me an extra cup he had in his locker (yeah, you heard me: a cup). David actually gave me his favorite pants—the ones he got during big-league camp. (David: I am an amazing brother. I had to wear clown-looking minor league pants so Jason could have big-league ones.)

Then there were the looks on the guys' faces as they came into the clubhouse and saw me suited up. It was priceless. The story captivated them as we talked about it in the locker room. It was hard for many of them to believe. For David and me, we were living a dream. Just twenty-four hours earlier I was in the stands watching my brother and his buddies play. Now I was in the locker room suiting up to take the field as a player on the team.

As I walked down the tunnel to take the field for batting practice, reality began to set in. *I haven't seen a live pitch or taken a ground ball in more than three months*, I thought to myself. That's a long time in the game of baseball where timing is everything. The only swings I had taken were the few with David a couple of days before, and I was still sore from those. So I figured I'd take it easy and lie low. But that wasn't going to happen—I was the talk of the team the minute I took the field. All the guys wanted to see a competition between David and me—who could throw farther, hit better, run faster, you name it. I let David win (I didn't want the guys to witness him cry).

That night we played the El Paso Diablos, the Double-A affiliate of the Arizona Diamondbacks. I had never been so excited to sit the bench in my entire life—I was just thrilled to be on the team. From my view, I had the best seat in the house. When I was with the O's, I hated riding the pine, but now I had a new perspective on the game. I was living the dream I had prayed about since we were young—to play on the same team with David in the pros. So whether I played or not, I wasn't going to miss any of it, like Dad said.

The next night I sat the bench again, but I did take a killer round of batting practice before the game. As a matter of fact, it was so good that Hammer took note. During BP, we played a hitting game where the pitching coach would try to strike us out. From such a short distance, he was making quick work of most of the hitters. But for some crazy reason I was crushing the ball. He couldn't strike me out. I was relaxed and having so much fun I felt like a kid again—there was no pressure to perform. So reacting to curveballs and change-ups didn't faze me at all. The players were whooping all around the cage the more I connected with pitches and drove them around the field. It was a blast.

David was right there with me on the bench that second night. (Is it just me, or is that a lot of bench sitting for David?) Chad Hutchinson—the guy from Stanford we mentioned earlier—was on the mound for us. In between innings I would jump up and run down the right field line to warm up our right fielder. It was wonderful to be out there in uniform under the lights of a Double-A park. I soaked up every minute of it, just like Dad had said.

Several times throughout the game, David would say, "Can you believe this? It's so surreal. This is just crazy."

Scenes from the past flashed through my mind as I sat there in the dugout. Thoughts of lying in a hospital room knowing I would probably never play again, hearing my manager release me from the O's, and walking up to the Travelers' stadium feeling like an average Joe all came rushing back to me. Yet now here I was, decked out in full uniform with my name officially on the roster of a Double-A team.

Signing with the Cardinals, suiting up in a uniform, taking batting practice on the field, and signing autographs again for the kids after a game was nothing short of a miracle. And if the story ended right there, it would stand as one of the most awe-inspiring acts of God in my life—a direct answer to prayer and the rebirth of my childhood dream. But that's not the end of the story. God had something else up His sleeve.

Nineteen

BREAK IT UP

I see great things in baseball. It's our game—the American game. It will . . . repair these losses, and be a blessing to us.

—Walt Whitman[1]

We got to the stadium on Wednesday and went through our normal pregame routine before taking the field for the final game against El Paso. It was Greek night at the ballpark that evening, with a ton of fraternity and sorority members from local colleges in attendance. Thousands of college kids were back in town from summer break, so the city was filled with youthful energy—and so was Ray Winder Field that night. Add to that the fact that it was the last game of the year in Little Rock, and it was a pretty raucous atmosphere with a jam-packed crowd.

The Diablos had a no-hitter going in the sixth inning. On the mound was this big, tall lefty. He was supposedly slated to go up to the big leagues after the game. His stuff was nasty, and none of our hitters could touch him. Our window of opportunity was closing, not just to win the game but also to avoid the embarrassment of not making a hit in front of one of our biggest crowds all year. We were both on the bench again that night, chewing sunflower seeds and enjoying all the crazy fans with the other players.

With two outs in the sixth inning and nobody on, Hammer yelled across the field from his third base coaching box, "Benham!" and pounded his fists together, giving the sign to pinch hit. I (David) stood up, grabbed my bat, and started walking toward the on-deck circle. With a left-handed pitcher on the mound, it only made sense that he wanted a right-handed batter to face him. For those not familiar with baseball, right-handed hitters see the ball from left-handed pitchers easier and vice versa. So anytime someone pinch hits, coaches typically hit righties versus lefties and lefties versus righties.

That's a lot to think about, but suffice it to say I am a righty, and the pitcher was a lefty. Naturally, I was being called to pinch hit. But without hesitation Hammer yelled back to the dugout, "No! Your brother!"

Jason's head popped up—his eyes as big as basketballs. He stared down at me with a look of total horror on his face. He sat there frozen for a few seconds before hopping up to his feet, frantically looking for his batting gloves, his bat, and a helmet. He yelled down to me, "Dude! I need your bat . . . and a helmet. And where are your batting gloves?"

Jason hadn't seen a live pitch in more than three months. He wasn't even expecting to play, much less pinch hit in a tight ball game in a jam-packed stadium against a tough lefty with a no-hit shutout on the line. This caught him totally off guard. I thought he might wet his pants.

I will never forget what took place in the dugout just before Jason went up to hit. He was frantically looking for a bat and helmet while all the guys were smacking him on the backside and yelling, "Go get 'em!" Once he found the bat he wanted to use, he walked to the top step of the dugout, turned around and looked at everyone on the bench, and with a broad smile on his face, he said, "Sit tight, boys. I'll be right back!"

We erupted in laughter. We knew what he was saying. It had been so long since he had seen a live pitch, and he was a lefty batter facing a tough lefty pitcher who was throwing gas—not to mention he was coming to the plate in the middle of a no-hit shutout—he knew he wasn't going to be up there long.

My legs were numb! Once I gathered my stuff and got my emotions under control, I remember walking up to the plate with an overwhelming sense of peace. It was as if everything started to go in slow motion. I wasn't nervous. I wasn't scared. I was actually having fun because I realized I had nothing to lose. If I got a hit or struck out, it didn't matter. The joy was in the process, not the result. I honestly felt like I was playing Wiffle ball in my front yard again. My dream of playing pro ball had been dead, and for months I had been trying to come to grips with the fact that I was done playing baseball. But now I had another miraculous chance. And I planned to make the most of it. I was going to swing for the fences.

As Jason walked up to the plate, I sat in the dugout replaying all of the momentous events in his life over the past few years:

Jason becoming a superstar during his senior year, getting drafted, breaking his leg, getting released, praying together in center field, signing a contract to play for Arkansas. And now I was watching him, as my teammate on a Double-A team in the Cardinals organization, walk up to the plate to hit. Unbelievable.

The stadium was thumping. "Cotton-Eyed Joe" was blaring over the speakers during Jason's approach to the plate. "Where did you come from? Where did you go? Where did you come from, Cotton-Eyed Joe?" It was hysterical watching the college kids jumping up and down to the music. It seemed as if every seat in the stadium was bouncing.

As Jason neared the plate, I quietly and discreetly slid off the bench, down onto one knee, and uttered a prayer.

"Lord Jesus, help him to make contact."

No one saw me as I was sitting on the far end of the bench. I was nervous for Jason and could barely watch, so I stayed on my knee, praying. I would have been happy if he simply made contact with the ball. Even a foul ball would have been fine. It would have been respectable and shown that he wasn't completely in over his head.

Jason walked up to the batter's box and drew a little cross in the dirt with his foot like he did every time he came to the plate. He dug in with his back foot. The El Paso pitcher came set and looked in for the sign, giving a quick nod to the first one. I knew what was coming—fastball. By this time in our lives, Jason and I had played hundreds of games together, and I knew what he was thinking up there: *The first pitch I see, I'm swinging.* If the pitcher threw the ball over the backstop, Jason would swing at it. So I prayed the pitcher would throw it right down the middle.

He went into his windup and fired a blazing fastball right down the middle of the plate.

Whack!

Jason unloaded on the ball and hit a missile to center field that bounced off the wall for a stand-up double, breaking up the no-hitter and sending our fans into an absolute frenzy. The guys in the dugout went nuts, jumping around and knocking me all around the dugout. It was like I had just gotten the hit. Most of them, including me, couldn't believe what just happened.

I looked out at second base, and there was Jason, standing with his hands on his hips, looking all around as bursting cheers from the crowd filled the Arkansas night. Just a few nights before he was sitting in the stands, and now he was standing on the field, in the game, claiming second base after a stand-up double to break up a no-hitter, in the last home game of the season. I felt like I was watching a movie.

With the momentum of Jason's hit, our next batter reached base as well. Then our first baseman hit a three-run homer to give us the lead. If the crowd was loud before, it was insane now. Jason was the first player to cross home plate and then turned to wait for the other two guys to cross before coming back to the dugout. As soon as he got to the top step, the guys attacked him. You would've thought he had hit the home run.

We won the game that night, and Jason was the spark that made it all happen.

The scene after the game was amazing—Jason standing over by the bleachers signing autographs and talking to the local media. Kids all around wanted his autograph while reporters wanted his interview. Only God could have orchestrated something like this. I sat in the dugout and just took it all in, whispering a quick prayer of thanks. "Lord Jesus, thank You. You are incredible! You direct our lives and grant us the desires of our hearts. Thank You so much for this."

After fifteen minutes of interviews and autographs, we walked into the clubhouse to shower and hit the spread. It's funny how much better the food is at the Double-A level than it is in Single A. We actually had meat and vegetables, and it was hot most of the time. All the players were still talking about Jason's hit. Before we could get our uniforms off, Hammer walked in with a quick announcement for the team.

"Hey, fellas, pack your bags for the road trip tomorrow," he said as he bit into a sandwich. "Shreveport's a long ride from here."

We both jerked to attention and looked at each other in total astonishment, overwhelmed by what we'd just heard. In all the excitement over Jason coming to Little Rock and signing to play with the team, I had not looked at the schedule to realize our last series of the year was against the Captains at Fair Grounds Field in Shreveport.

Are you kidding?!

There is absolutely no way this was an accident, and we don't believe in coincidences. This was nothing less than the hand of the living God working behind the scenes to orchestrate events in such a way as to produce an outcome we never could have scripted. The thoughts and memories rushed through my mind as I tried to process what I had just heard. The 4:30 a.m. rides in our station wagon down I-20 past the stadium. Dad whispering for us to wake up, praying we would play there together one day. College trips as we passed through Shreveport, praying the same.

And now it was all coming true.

You cannot make this stuff up. How could something like this happen unless God Himself makes it happen?

I felt so overwhelmed I almost lost it right there in the clubhouse. "Dude, we're going to Shreveport!" I said to Jason as my voice started shaking. "I had no idea! I didn't look at the schedule."

We were both so overcome with gratitude we were weak in the knees. God's miracles were coming so fast, and His goodness was so abundant, we couldn't keep up.

We just sat there next to each other at our lockers as all the other guys were packing their bags for the trip, without saying a word, just taking it all in—fully experiencing the moment God was giving us. There is no way to explain it other than to say we were living in the middle of a miracle.

When we got back to the house, the first thing we did was call Dad to tell him the news—not just that Jason had gotten a hit, broken up a no-hitter, and started a game-winning rally, but that we were headed to Shreveport.

"Boys, I know. I already looked at the schedule," he responded. Then he offered an eternal perspective to what was going on in our lives: "I'm in awe right now for how good God has been to you both. And I am so proud of you. Not only did you pray and trust God to make your dream a reality, but you also honored Him in the process. God promises that if you honor Him, He will honor you. Do you remember the way you boys chose not to play on Sundays in Little League and in high school even when you didn't quite understand why? God saw that. And when you chose to share the gospel after games in college? God saw that. You're both now walking in the midst of His favor. So enjoy it, and we'll see you in Shreveport—along with a whole bunch of your friends and family!"

Mom then jumped on the phone and informed us of everyone coming, including Tori, who had flown in a few days earlier. Several of our friends and old coaches were set to come as well—once they all found out we were playing in Shreveport together, everyone wanted to see us.

The next morning we arrived at the stadium for a three-hour trip to Shreveport and a date with our lifelong dream.

SHREVEPORT

When you cease to dream you cease to live.

—Malcolm Forbes[1]

We got to the ballpark early, at 9 a.m., as everyone was loading the bus. Since Jason was going back to Texas after the series to be with Tori, he had to drive his truck to Shreveport, so I asked Hammer if I could ride with him. Thankfully, he let me go.

Before leaving the parking lot, we paused to pray. This time, instead of *asking* God to make our Shreveport dream come true, we *thanked* Him for making it happen. We thought of all the years Dad woke us up on our summer trips as little-leaguers to pray for this and of all the times we'd passed by the stadium as college players, praying for the same. Now, here we were, professional baseball players on the same team headed to Shreveport for a four-game series. Only God could have done this.

"Can you really believe this is happening?" I said to Jason after we finished praying.

"It feels too good to be true," he responded. "It's like we're living in a fairy tale."

As we made our way down the road to Shreveport, we thought of Dad—how he'd continued to cultivate the dream in us as kids, of one day playing in this stadium. "Wouldn't it be great if . . . ?" We had asked ourselves that question countless times over the years, clinging to that hope during the times when it seemed impossible. And now here we were, driving down the highway, living out its reality.

It was the longest three-hour trip of our lives. We couldn't get there fast enough. For the rest of our teammates, it was just another road trip. But for us, it was our dream come true.

We arrived in town and stopped at the team hotel, just a few miles from the stadium. Batting practice was canceled because it was a travel day, so the team didn't have to be at the field until 6:00 for a 7:30 p.m. game. But Jason and I weren't about to wait that long—we couldn't wait to walk out onto the grass and see the inside of the stadium we'd prayed about for years.

We jumped back in the truck and headed to Fair Grounds Field—about three hours before game time—hoping we'd find a gate that was open. As we pulled into the parking lot, we recalled all the times we wanted to go inside and see a game but didn't, holding on to the hope that one day we'd be there as players. Fortunately the gate to the players' entrance was open, so we made our way to the visitors' clubhouse and walked into a room full of empty lockers. As we stood there looking around, taking it all in, we saw a sign that read "To the Field" and a long tunnel leading to the dugout.

"Dude, let's go!" Jason said, pointing to the sign. So we threw our bags into a couple of lockers and walked toward the light at the end of the tunnel. As we neared the entrance to the dugout, we saw steps leading up to the field. When we walked onto the field, we just stood there, taking in all the sights, sounds, and smells of the place we had dreamed about for so long. This was our Yankee Stadium—our "field of dreams." This was our "big show" that Grampa had referenced in his last words to us.

We were both thinking the same thing—*Wow. We made it. We actually made it.* Neither one of us said a word; we just stood there and embraced the moment.

Then, as if on cue, we both walked directly toward the outfield. We're pretty sure the grounds crew thought we were crazy when we dropped to our knees in center field and prayed to God.

"Lord Jesus, thank You! We know You have done this, not just for us, but so that we will forever have a testimony of Your mighty power. What is impossible with man is possible with You. All those years we prayed for this day, and little did we know You were behind the scenes, putting the pieces together to make it happen. You are an amazing God. We love You. Thank You!"

As soon as we finished praying, we stood up, turned around, and there in the upper deck was our dad, standing with his arms raised high in the air, praising the Lord. He'd found a way into the stadium and was able to see us pray in the outfield. He couldn't make it down to us on the field, but he was with us in spirit, thanking the same God who'd made it all happen.

It felt good to see Dad filled with so much joy. He was the one who had taught us to love God, to follow His commands, to dream big, to work hard, to serve those around us, to use our gifts for God's glory, to be faithful in little things, and to trust the Lord with our future. He was the man who had instilled in us, so many years before, the very dream that was coming true before his eyes.

As we made our way back toward the dugout, Dad came down to the field. "Boys," he said, "never forget how powerful and faithful God is to those who put their faith, hope, and trust in Him. He is always working behind the scenes. Even if we don't think He's working, He is. And when it seems He's not listening, He is. Because He is faithful. He heard our prayers all those years ago, and now we're seeing His answer in a very special way."

About that time Mom walked in with our little brother and sister, and my (Jason's) heart skipped a beat when I saw Tori was with them. Unfortunately David and I couldn't stay long with the family because we had some baseball to play. So we hugged everybody and headed back down to the clubhouse. We had to get ready for a four-game set against the Captains to cap off the 2000 season.

That night the Captains had a nasty pitcher who shut us down, giving up three hits and striking out eleven in seven innings. When they brought in their closer, Hammer signaled for me to pinch hit again. Of course, I was again shocked that he called on me, just as I was the night before. I didn't expect to get another chance to play, but Hammer wanted to try his luck on me one more time. Thankfully, I had my gear close by, so I grabbed my bat and headed to the plate.

The interesting part of the story is that the closer for Shreveport was one of our teammates back at Liberty, Benji

Miller. He and I looked at each other as I walked up to the plate, trying to hold back our smiles. Back in the day, at Liberty, when we'd play intra-squad games, Benji discovered I was a sucker for the low outside change-up. He ate me alive with that pitch in college. So of all the times I didn't want to face Benji, it was this night—my first at bat in the Shreveport stadium where I had dreamed of playing ever since I was a kid. God has a sense of humor.

I made my traditional cross in the dirt with my right foot, stepped into the box, and dug in for my second plate appearance as a Cardinal. Benji reared back and let it loose. Just as I had suspected, it was a low and away change-up. But this time I was waiting for it and drove a line drive over the shortstop's head for a single. I rounded first and headed back to the bag, thinking to myself, *I can't believe I just did that—I finally hit that pitch!* As I stood on first, I gave a little wink to Benji when he looked over. Not only had I finally gotten the best of him, but I was 2 for 2 as a Cardinal.

Fortunately for Benji, but unfortunately for our team, he ended up mowing down the rest of our hitters, handing us our first loss of the series. Afterward we went out to eat with our family and invited Benji to come along. He laughed pretty hard when I said, "Dude, why did you throw that pitch? You knew I was waiting for it! That was payback for what you did to me at Liberty."

Our game the next night was a thriller. We were tied at 2 in the seventh when the Captains pushed across a run. We answered in the top of the eighth with two runs to take a 4-3 lead, but Shreveport came back in the bottom of the inning to tie the score at 4.

In the top of the ninth, Hammer yelled again into the dugout, "Benham!" pointing to me. He was looking for a ninth-inning rally, and it seemed that David was not the guy for the job. (Sorry, dude. I just had to go there.)

Interestingly, not only was I becoming the go-to pinch-hitter for the team, but Benji was on the mound again! *I know what he's going to throw for the first pitch*, I thought as I walked out to the plate, unable to keep the smile off my face. "But I'm not going to swing at it—I am going to wait until he throws a fastball."

Sure enough, he did it again—first pitch change-up, low and outside. I almost bit the bait and swung at it, but I held back. Ball one. The next pitch was a 92-mile-per-hour fastball on the inside of the plate—just what I was waiting for. *Whack!* I turned on it and roped it to right field for another single. I still remember how good that one felt.

As I rounded first base, I started laughing to myself. Not only was I playing professional baseball again, with David, in Shreveport, but now I had three base hits on three pitches—two off my college teammate—and I was batting 1.000 in Double A! I could get used to this.

The next hitter laid down a bunt that advanced me to second. At this point I started to get a little nervous. While I was feeling more comfortable at the plate, I hadn't sprinted in over three months. The thought of running full speed if the next batter got a hit made me nervous.

As God would have it, our next hitter lined a base hit to right field. I took off toward third, barely able to feel my legs. Hammer was yelling, "You better run, boy!" As I rounded the bag, I felt as though I hit quicksand.

David was laughing hysterically in the dugout because he

knew my hips and hamstrings were tight from not sprinting in several months. Later he told me it looked like I had cinder blocks around my ankles. When I rounded the bag, it was as if I'd hit a 100-mile-per-hour headwind. My back straightened up and my head was cocked back—I was giving it all I had.

The right fielder got the ball and came up throwing. I barreled toward home as our on-deck hitter stood at the plate waving his arms and yelling, "Get down!" I dove toward the plate, sliding headfirst as the catcher grabbed the ball and swiped the tag. A big cloud of dust swirled around us as we waited for the umpire's call.

"Safe!"

I rolled over and felt as if I had just run a 400-meter sprint. My legs were shot. I slowly got up, brushing off the front of my uniform, thanking God the piano on my back didn't slow me down enough to lose the game. My teammates mauled me in the dugout with helmet smacks and butt slaps. With that run, we took home the victory.

But the fun didn't stop there. The next day we walked into the clubhouse and looked at the lineup card posted on the wall—I was in the starting lineup at second base. David was, too, playing catcher. We both just stared at the lineup card. When I signed, I was happy to sit on the bench and enjoy the rest of the season as a part of the team. But then I became our best pinch-hitter. And now I had earned a spot in the starting lineup—with David. But not only that. We were both starting for the same team in the same stadium we had prayed to play in since we were kids. And our family was there to watch it all.

Only God.

Neither of us got a hit that game. The only highlight was

when a sky-high fly ball was hit to me at second base—I did a 360 turn before catching it, falling backward onto my back. Evidently it was quite a sight to see. When I came into the dugout, one of the guys said, "Get a map, Magellan!" (There's always time for some good baseball banter.)

Our fourth game of the series was the last game of the season, and I was in the starting lineup again at second base. This time, by God's amazing grace, I made the most of my appearances at the plate, going 3-for-5 and driving in one run in a 6-2 win.

In my final at bat, I faced a lefty who had a nasty curveball. I knew this could potentially be my last at bat in professional baseball, as the Cards had only signed me through the end of the season. After two curveballs in a row, he threw an inside fastball that I laced down the right field line for a stand-up double—a fitting end to a miraculous run.

The game ended, and the season was over. Not only did David and I fulfill our lifelong dream together, but I played better than I had played in a long time. In five games, I had gone 6-for-11 (a .545 batting average) with two doubles, an RBI, and three runs scored. That performance was good enough to earn me runner-up honors for the Texas League Player of the Week. It was just crazy.

What a moment it was, walking out of the stadium after that last game with Jason and our family gathered around us, talking and reminiscing about what a miraculous experience this truly was. It wasn't a dream fulfilled just for the two of us but a dream our entire family enjoyed together. God had resurrected Jason's career to make this dream a reality for us all. Watching him play so well was just icing on the cake.

"Hey, guys," Dad said before we piled into our cars to head back home to Garland. "Just think about all the times we drove past this place and prayed for this to happen." We glanced toward the highway as the cars whisked by, remembering the prayers we prayed traveling down that same road. "You now have a testimony that you'll carry the rest of your lives, reminding you of God's faithfulness, His working behind the scenes proving He can be trusted to put the pieces of your story in place, in His time, and in His way."

And with that, we loaded up and headed down I-20 for a three-hour road trip home. Our time in Shreveport had come to an end—a very happy ending indeed.

Epilogue

As if things couldn't get any better for me (Jason), that December Tori and I got married and began our life together. That was two dreams come true for me in a matter of months—not a bad year.

For our honeymoon, we stayed in South Beach for a few days before going on a cruise to the Bahamas. As we packed to leave the hotel for the cruise ship, I got a call from my former agent.

"Hey, Jason, we've been trying to get in touch with you," he said. "The Cardinals want to know where they can send your contract."

"Do what?" I responded in shock. "They want to sign me again?"

"Yes, sir," he responded. "They were impressed with what you did back in August and want to bring you back."

Wow—that felt good to hear. They wanted me back—like, to play in Double A, with a chance at the big leagues. *I could do this*, I thought after hanging up. *Maybe I'll stay hot at the plate, and just maybe I could make it to the show.* But then I looked over at my new bride and realized how difficult it would be for her if I were on the road all the time chasing my dream.

While I was excited about the idea of playing again and honored the Cardinals wanted to sign me, the offer actually threw me a curveball. I had already lined up jobs for Tori and me in Atlanta with John Maxwell's leadership company, the Injoy Group, since I didn't know the Cardinals wanted me back. I was now faced with a difficult decision—leave her and pursue my dream or stay with her and begin a new chapter in life.

Tori sat next to me while I was on the phone, anxiously waiting for me to tell her what was going on. "The Cardinals offered me a contract for next season," I told her.

"Well, then you should sign," she immediately responded. "This has always been your lifelong dream, and I think you should pursue it."

The phone call from my agent had felt good, but Tori's response felt even better. To know that she was willing to put up with Minor League life for me was truly a blessing.

"I told him I would pray about it and get back with him in a few weeks," I said.

For almost our entire honeymoon we talked about what life would be like for us if I signed. I did not realize what a struggle that phone call would turn out to be for me. I wanted to play again, especially on the same team as David. But I also wanted to be with Tori, and I didn't want to jeopardize the opportunity we had to work together. Sharing a job with her at the same company was an investment I wanted to make in our marriage.

To make the decision even more difficult, when we arrived in Atlanta after our honeymoon, my boss—who happened to be a college friend from Liberty—said he fully supported my decision to play again; he'd even allow Tori to keep her job while I was on the road. He also said he'd try to give mine back if things didn't work out in baseball.

Man, that's a tough offer to turn down.

There wasn't a time in my life when I was more torn over what to do. I was uncertain which direction to take, yet the more I prayed about it, the more it became clear. God gave me a specific word one morning before I left for work as I prayed about it in the living room of our apartment—when your dream costs more than you're willing to pay, it's time to let it go.

Signing with the Cardinals would have meant leaving Tori in Atlanta, uprooting myself and traveling who knows where, and walking away from a good job (a mature step I needed to take as a man). My heart was more inclined toward Tori and building a family with her than it was toward baseball, so I made the decision to walk away from the game once and for all.

Later that day I called the Cardinals to tell them my decision. I still remember sitting in my cubicle at the office with my headset on, talking to the same minor league coordinator who'd signed me the previous summer. I told him how grateful I was for the offer and how much I wanted to play, but then I told him I couldn't accept his offer and explained my reason for declining.

I wasn't sure how he would respond—not many guys turn down a contract offer from a major league club, but he told me he respected my decision and wished me the best.

I hung up the phone, and at that moment I realized I had also just officially hung up my cleats. Tears started rolling down my cheeks as I tried to hide my emotions from my coworkers. Tori saw me and came to put her arm around me. This hurt her as much as it did me. But I know deep down she was thankful to see that I had chosen *our* dream instead of just *my* dream.

Although I felt divine contentment about it, that decision was one of the hardest I've had to make. The most difficult part of it all was giving up the identity of being a professional baseball player. For the next several months I was cooped up in a cubicle, wearing a headset and living the life of an average Joe in the workplace. It was there I learned what it meant to worship God through my work. God taught me to find my identity in who I *am*, not in what I *do*. All I had to do was be faithful right where He placed me—whether on a baseball diamond or in an office cube.

And with that, I said goodbye to baseball and left the dream in David's hands to carry for us both.

I was invited back to Major League spring training with the Cardinals the following season, in 2001. It was the first baseball season that I knew Jason was out of the game for good. Playing baseball had always been our dream together. So with him not in the game anymore, I didn't have the same burn and desire I once had.

I was assigned again that year to the Double-A team, which had moved from Arkansas to New Haven, Connecticut. The thrill of playing in Arkansas with Jason and then together in Shreveport so deeply satisfied me that playing another full season didn't carry the same excitement it once had. Looking back, I realize I lost my edge a bit. I didn't play bad, but I wasn't lighting it up either.

My family continued to grow; Lori was pregnant with our second son, Ty, at the time; and with Jason telling me "normal life" wasn't that bad, I continued to grow more disenchanted with the game. Slogging around in the minors wasn't worth the cost it once was—especially for my wife.

By late July I had lost most of my interest in the game. With about six weeks left in the season, we were playing in Norwich, Connecticut, against the Yankees Double-A team when I looked up from the on-deck circle during the game and saw Lori chasing my son, Bailey, around the stadium. She was eight months pregnant and exhausted. I knew we couldn't keep this up. That's when the dream finally died in my heart. I learned the same lesson Jason had learned several months before—my dream was now costing more than I was willing to pay, and Lori was paying the price. It was time to let it go.

I finished out the season and then asked the Cardinals for my release, which they gave me. Then I called my agent.

"I'm done, man," I said when he answered the phone. "It's just too much for my family; and Jason's out of the game now, too, so I don't want it as bad."

"But you were on the fast track just a few years ago, bro," he responded. "How about you let me make a few phone calls to other teams and get back to you before you make your final decision?" he said.

I told him I'd pray about it for a few days with Lori, and he could call me back if he wanted. Two days later he called.

"The Rockies want to sign you. I believe you can make it to the big leagues with these guys, David," he said. "Let's give it a shot."

But I didn't want to play anymore. The dream was dead. By this time Jason had moved to North Carolina to be a corporate chaplain, and he had already convinced me to join him there. Lori and I felt the Lord wanted us to step away from the game, so I simply thanked my agent and declined the offer.

I bade my farewell to baseball, with a grateful heart for the opportunities I'd been given in the game, and called it a career. The end of the previous season in Shreveport with Jason was good enough for me. It was time to move on.

My first job out of pro ball was actually as a janitor at a Christian school. Jason got me the job. There I learned the same lesson Jason had learned—my identity is found not in what I do but in who I am. My one role was to be faithful right where God had placed me and bring Him glory whether holding a baseball bat or a broomstick. It was a tough lesson but a necessary one— one that all men need.

But for Jason and me, we walked away from the game with hearts that were full. We had accomplished a childhood dream and had seen the miraculous hand of God working in ways we never imagined possible. We had dreamed together, worked together, prayed together, played together, celebrated together, and grown together. And now we would move on with our lives—together.

Although we never made it to the big leagues, we knew we would always have Shreveport—a testimony of God's faithfulness and a constant reminder that even when we don't know what God is up to, He is always working behind the scenes, putting the pieces of our puzzle together.

So don't be discouraged when it may seem your life is not what you want it to be and you wonder if God is doing anything about it. He is. Trust that His ways are higher than our ways and know that He is perfectly capable of giving you a story to cling to in your most desperate hours.

God is building a testimony for you—one that not only will become a reminder of God's faithfulness in your life but also will be a powerful weapon to pull you through the diffi-cult time you may be going through. Trust Him. He is weaving the fabric of *your* story into the canvas of *His*tory. He's putting the pieces of *your* puzzle together.

You can trust Him. The question is, will you?

APPENDIX

Article from the *Dallas Morning News*

SECOND NATURE: JASON BENHAM HAS ACCEPTED LIVING IN BASEBALL SHADOW OF TWIN, DAVID. NOW, THEY FINALLY GO SEPARATE WAYS

By Kevin Sherrington, Staff Writer of the *Dallas Morning News* Published: June 7, 1998 (Reprinted with permission.)

Every day, for 22 years, you wake up in a room with him. He looks just like you. He walks like you, talks like you, thinks like you. Even friends can't always tell you apart. Until you get on a baseball field, that is, and then it's obvious.

He's better than you.

Not a little bit better. A lot better. The pros drafted him, not you, and you sat in a church and cried. Two years later, they drafted him again and passed on you again. It still hurt, but you were resigned to it.

You had to be. Even after this season at Liberty University, when you outplayed your brother for the first time in your life, when you were the MVP of the Big South Conference, even then you didn't forget who was really better.

You don't forget if you're Jason Benham. Not if your twin brother, David, is maybe the best college catcher in the country.

You can't forget. Not when even your father won't let you.

"Who's better?" Flip Benham asks Jason.

"Better at what?" Jason asks his dad, afraid of the answer.

"Baseball," Flip says.

Faye Benham knows the answer. She also knows it doesn't need to be asked, not here, late one night in Florida in front of family, friends, and strangers, and she tells her husband as much.

Still, it hangs out there like a lazy fly ball that won't fall out of the summer sky.

Who's better?

"David is," Jason says, and shrugs.

You could resent it. You worked just as hard as he did to be the best. Since you were 15, the two of you got up every morning before dawn and did those crazy workouts, hopping on one leg, then the other, then both.

You were good, but he was better, at everything. He is two minutes older, an inch taller, two-tenths of a grade point smarter. He always played the more pivotal position. You played tailback, but he was the quarterback. You played forward, but he was the point guard.

You play third base. He's the catcher.

How could you be so alike, and yet so different? You're so close that all it takes is a look from third base and your brother reads it and throws a laser to pick off a runner.

But he's the prospect, not you. You could have resented him for that difference. You could have, but then you wouldn't be Jason Benham.

You wouldn't be the brother who looked out for David every day, who kept up with his wallet and keys and kept him out of trouble, the brother who ran with him and worked with him and prayed with him.

The brother who never left him.

"We shared a womb," Jason says, "and we shared a room."

Every day, for 22 years. Now, it is almost over. All that's left, after more than 1,500 baseball games together, is an NCAA regional in Tallahassee, Fla.

The Benham twins' last game.

Faye Benham didn't know she was having twins until a week before delivery, and she didn't feel twice blessed.

"I thought it was going to be terrible," she says. "I already had one little girl who was 3, and now I'm going to have twin boys."

The concern seems odd now. Fourteen years after her twins, she had another girl. Then, two years later, another boy. Children, theirs and others, would become the center of the Benhams' lives. Faye's husband, Flip, is national director of Operation Rescue National, perhaps the nation's most high-profile anti-abortion group.

But, before he became famous for getting arrested, Flip was just a Methodist minister in Garland who reared his boys on prayer, platitudes.

He gave them the indoctrination when they were 5 years old. Noticing how athletic they were in backyard games, he told them they were going to play in a flag football league.

"You guys have a gift," Flip told them, "and the Lord will honor your gift."

And that's when the boys started crying.

A kindly coach helped them get over it. Rick Williams

coached them in football and their first year of baseball. It was Williams who made Jason a left-handed hitter. Jason was having some trouble hitting, but that's not the reason for the switch.

After that first year, Flip coached the boys in baseball until high school. Not that he knew much about the sport.

"Nothing," David says.

"Not a thing," says Jason.

They say he taught them bigger lessons. He told them it was just as important to conduct yourself properly as win, and he taught his boys the value of hard work.

Flip didn't know much about baseball, but he had a good arm. He'd get in the backyard for batting practice and throw tennis balls as hard as he could.

He had a good arm, not an accurate one. Half the time, he'd drill the boys, which sickened Faye.

This is where Jason picks up the narrative. Most of the time, David does all the talking. Once during an interview, Jason asks his brother, "Do you want me to answer?" Maybe this acquiescence is a result of always coming in second, as if he's not as qualified to speak. But it is only a small concession. David is the talker, but Jason is the wit, and it is as subtle as a stop sign. David will be rolling along, chewing up conversation when Jason suddenly cuts in and asks a stranger about his dentures.

Dentures?

Anyway, Jason takes over now from his brother when it comes time to play the part of his parents in backyard batting practice.

Mom (high, panicky voice): "Oh, oh, you're going to hurt them. Stop it, stop it."

Dad (think W. C. Fields): "Quiet, Faye, this is the only way they'll learn."

Flip was always out in the backyard with his boys, making men of them. The sport didn't matter: baseball, basketball, Wiffle ball.

Boxing. Jason mimics his dad—hands up, head moving side to side as he watches his boys whaling away at each other.

Mom (same voice): "Oh, oh, they're going to get hurt. Stop it, stop it."

Dad (distracted): "Quiet, Faye, let 'em hit each other."

Flip taught the twins lots of things, some not so good. One was a submarine pitch, a quasi-underhanded throw. Flip demonstrated, then nodded at David.

"All right," he said, "now see if you can do it."

David gave it all he had. Starting low, the ball quickly rose over Flip's glove and the eave of their house, gathering speed on its errant journey until it zeroed in on the neighbors' bedroom window, delivering a 6:15 wake-up call.

The day Faye Benham announced she was pregnant with a third son, those same neighbors put their house on the market. On the day they moved out, they told the Benhams, "We should have done this years ago."

Faye was nonplussed. "Don't go," she told them, "we've just broken you in."

The Benham boys broke lots of things, prompting years of unexpected callers at the front door.

Neighbor: "Do you know what your boys did?"

Faye: "Whatever it was, I'm sorry. I can't do anything with them. Talk to their father."

David got most of the whippings. "If anyone was going to buck the establishment," Faye says, "it was David."

So it was Jason who took it upon himself to keep his brother out of trouble. When David would sneak out of the house to see his girlfriend, Jason tried to stop him, provoking the only fights the brothers have ever had.

The impasse never lasted long. They were a team. They showed up that way in *Sports Illustrated*, in the Faces in the Crowd section, when their eighth-grade football team at Garland Christian Academy went 10-0 and their basketball team finished 19-1.

No goal was too high, not even a basketball rim. On Christmas Eve of their freshman year, they promised they would dunk a basketball before the school year was over. At the time, David was 5-9 and Jason was 5-8. Neither could jump higher than the middle of the net. So the boys and a friend came up with a workout program requiring knee bends, calf raises and hopping.

Lots of hopping. Every morning but Sunday, they got up at 5:30 to train. Neighbors' headlights would find the boys hopping 100 yards down the street, first on one leg, then the other, then both.

Three weeks after the workouts started, both could grab the rim. In three months, they could dunk a tennis ball.

And, on April 17, 1991, six weeks before deadline, both dunked a basketball. First David, then Jason.

"The whole thing put the stamp of approval on it," Jason says, "that hard work will pay off."

They learned that lesson again as seniors at GCA, a school so small it didn't even have a baseball field. Figuring no recruiters would see them, the twins asked their father about transferring to North Garland High School.

Flip said no. "A man's gift will make his way," he told them.

A few weeks later, a former pastor and major league player recommended the twins to Collegiate Baseball, which ranked them in its top 50 recruits. Liberty's baseball coach contacted them soon after and offered a full scholarship to each.

Other schools solicited them, too. The New York Mets drafted David in the 65th round and offered him a $12,000 bonus.

He said no. He chose Liberty because he considered it the only evangelical school with an NCAA Division I baseball program. And he wanted to stay with Jason, who made him work harder than he would on his own.

"Everyone needs that someone who knows you inside out," Jason says.

"We really pushed each other," says David.

The twins figured they had pushed too far when they met Liberty's strength coach, Dave Williams. After sneaking on the football field at 6 a.m. to run wind sprints, they were scrambling back over the fence when the coaching staff informed them they wouldn't be prosecuted for trespassing.

Williams says their work ethic is the best he has seen, and he has worked at Texas A&M and Alabama. David is 6-2 and 195 pounds, and Jason is 6-1, 190. Their body fat is about 3.7 percent, half that of a good defensive back.

"One of the things I've had to teach them is how to rest," Williams says. "That's not in their vocabulary. It's work, work, work."

They work so hard that Williams once recommended them to football coach Sam Rutigliano, who considered offering a scholarship. "I'd just like to have their influence on the football team, if nothing else," Williams says.

They never let up. Their favorite food is an M&M Blizzard, a dairy treat they don't enjoy often because they consider it anathema to their workout regime, not to mention their rather vain commitment to washboard abs.

But if one twin won't indulge in a Blizzard, neither will the other.

David always orders first. "If he gets chicken," Jason says, "I'll just say, 'Make that two.'"

They share the same clothes, the same truck, the same room, home or away. They took all the same classes and graduated on time, each with a degree in history.

They share bunk beds in their apartment, just as they did at home. Jason, who has written a year's worth of daily devotionals he hopes to have published, leaves messages on the underside of his bunk for his brother.

Nothing too inspirational. "Usually, something like, 'Hello, buttface,'" Jason says.

David returns the sentiments. Last summer, "the best summer of our lives," David says, they played in a wooden bat league in Torrington, Conn. Once, just for the introduction of lineups, they switched jerseys. Jason ran out in his brother's jersey and shin guards.

When Jason's name was announced, David bounded out of the dugout, tripped and fell flat on his face.

"On purpose," Jason says.

There was no mistaking their play, though. David confirmed his potential as a pro prospect at Liberty. In 52 games his junior season, he hit .384 with seven home runs and 40 runs batted in.

Meanwhile, Jason hit .308 with three home runs and 28 RBIs.

What impressed scouts more, though, was David's "plus" arm. Flames pitching coach Randy Tomlin, who pitched five seasons for the Pittsburgh Pirates, says David's arm is as good as most catchers in the major leagues.

The Mets drafted David again after his junior season, this time in the 41st round. Everyone passed on Jason.

"My heart was broken when I wasn't drafted," Jason says. "The Lord took me through a lot. He got me to a point that I said, 'If you don't want me to play baseball anymore, that's fine.'

"The Lord had to teach me to be a man before I was a baseball player."

That lesson came this season. His coach, David Pastors, says Jason became a more patient hitter as he hit .426 with 11 home runs and 52 RBIs.

"I was real happy for Jason, too," Williams says. "All this time, he never resented his brother for all the things he's done. Now he's done well, too, and that makes it that much sweeter."

Jason considers it all providence.

"We can't take credit for any of it," he says. "None of it. Life just can't get any better."

But life changes, a difficult concept when you haven't lived much of it. David is getting married this September. Even if he weren't, baseball, which has kept the twins a team these past four years, will take them in separate directions soon.

Pastors wonders how they will handle that, not having each other to rely on for the first time.

"I asked them what they think it will be like when they won't be together anymore," he says.

"They both just looked at me."

Baseball is a game of signs and how to steal them. Coaches

give signs from the third base box and dugout, catchers signal pitchers, coaches signal outfielders, middle infielders signal each other.

The secret is not to give it away. The Benham twins never have, and for good reason.

They don't know what it is, either.

"I can look at him," David says, "and I just know I'm supposed to throw it."

Back in the Big South, no one could do anything about it. The Benhams probably ran the third base pickoff 50 times over the past four years, and still no one knew when it was coming. Once this season, with a runner at third, Winthrop's third base coach set up in a stance that allowed him to stare directly into Jason's face.

He was still studying Jason's expression when the umpire called out his runner.

In the first round of the double-elimination NCAA regional, the Benhams' sign and pickoff in the fourth inning proves to be the highlight of a 10-7 loss to top-seeded Florida State. The loss means the game the next day against Auburn could be their last, a point the twins don't like to discuss.

They aren't outwardly nostalgic. "You can't look back," David says, "and let the future escape."

But, an hour after the Florida State loss, in a restaurant where his father just made him confess who is the better player, Jason is asked to consider what it will be like to play without David.

Unlike David, Jason never has had a steady girlfriend. The closest relationship he has ever had is with his twin. David even called their relationship something like a marriage.

Jason has no flip answer now though. He looks at the table,

then turns just enough so no one else will hear. "I'll just take care of myself now," he says.

No one doubts he will. Or David, either. Friends, teammates and coaches marvel at their maturity, their ability to express themselves to audiences as large as a student assembly or as intimate as the man standing in the third base coach's box.

Flip Benham, says gab is their real gift, not baseball. "This is the platform," he says, pointing to the field from the top of the aluminum bleachers at Dick Howser Stadium.

From here, trying to catch a stray breeze in the noon sun, Flip will watch his sons play what will prove to be the best game of the regional. The game goes into the ninth inning, 2-2. David has thrown out a base runner in the third, and Jason's diving stop ended a threat in the seventh with runners at second and third.

Then, in the ninth, it comes undone. With a runner at second and two outs, Auburn's Chad Wandall hits a routine grounder to third base. The ball bounds toward Jason like a puppy. Just as it reaches him, he pulls up his glove, just a hair, and the ball scoots under and into left field, and the run scores.

The error is devastating. But, in what seems like providence in the bottom of the ninth, Jason has a chance to make it up. He comes to bat with the bases loaded and two outs.

As he steps to the plate and goes into his stance, not quite the mirror image of his brother, his hands higher and his body more relaxed, he is praying out loud.

"Me and you, Jesus," he says. "Me and you."

The last time he said that prayer, he hit a home run.

This time, he takes one pitch, then grounds into a fielder's choice.

And that's how his college career ends. Four-six, fielder's

choice. No heroics, no redemption, no last chance to prove everyone wrong.

Who's better, Jason?

Even people who love you don't always say the right thing. A thick-chested fan pulls him tight and says, "The Lord is so good to us, isn't he?"

Jason pulls away. "It doesn't always seem like it," he says, softly.

But it is only a momentary slip. In a few minutes, he talks about lessons learned, a maturity that Liberty pitcher Tim Harrell has come to expect.

"They've come a long way in four years," he says outside the stadium. "I've seen 'em grow into men I respect, men of morals and values. Of course, they're great ballplayers, and they're my friends."

He thinks a moment.

"I love 'em," he says, and smiles.

The sentiment is offered as a means of saying it's all right. It doesn't matter that Jason's error ended the season, Harrell is saying. No one cares about that now. All anyone wants to do—friends, fans, coaches, sports writers—is take care of Jason. They shake his hand, pull him close, maybe whisper something in his ear.

Florida State's third base coach sees Flip consoling Jason. "That's a great man right there," he tells Flip.

"A broken man right now," Flip says, "But you're right. He is a great man."

And David? He seems a little lost, what with all the attention on Jason. The poignancy of this last game together is lost on both twins, maybe because of the way it ended. The draft will wring all the emotion out of it two weeks later, when baseball makes it official they no longer will be a team: The Boston Red Sox will draft David in the 12th round and Baltimore will take Jason in the 37th.

Baseball still doesn't hold them as equals, but the dream runs on. Only now, as they give chase on those early-morning runs, all each will hear in the stillness is a solitary set of footsteps.

It will take some getting used to closing out 22 years and 1,500 games. After the last one, David got an idea of what it will be like as he walked off the field, his head swinging from side to side.

"Where'd Jason go?" he wondered aloud, probably not for the last time.

NOTES

INTRODUCTION

1. John Piper, "Every Moment in 2013 God Will Be Doing 10,000 Things in Your Life," DesiringGod.org, January 1, 2013, http://www.desiringgod.org/articles/every-moment-in-2013-god -will-be-doing-10-000-things-in-your-life.

CHAPTER 1: THE BIRTH OF A DREAM

1. *Field of Dreams*, film, directed by Phil Alden Robinson (Universal City, CA: Universal Studios, 1989).
2. *The Natural*, film, directed by Barry Levinson (Culver City, CA: Tristar Pictures, 1984).

CHAPTER 2: THE STADIUM OFF I-20

1. "There Used to Be a Ballpark," written by Joe Raposo and recorded by Frank Sinatra; reprinted with permission.
2. Brett Mandel, *Minor Players, Major Dreams* (Lincoln: University of Nebraska Press, 1997), 2.

CHAPTER 3: LITTLE LEAGUE LIFE

1. Paul Dickson, *Baseball's Greatest Quotations* (New York: Collins, 2008), 57.
2. "Relationships—Rules Without Relationships Lead to Rebellion," YouTube video, 2:27, parenting wisdom posted by

Josh McDowell, November 16, 2010, https://www.youtube.com/watch?v=Tx1SOiawASw.

CHAPTER 4: IN THE NEWS

1. Paul Dickson, *Baseball's Greatest Quotations* (New York: Collins, 2008), 598.
2. "Faces in the Crowd," *Sports Illustrated*, May 7, 1990, 85.

CHAPTER 5: A JAILHOUSE PRAYER

1. John Wesley, quoted in James W. Goll, *The Lifestyle of a Watchman: A 21-Day Journey to Becoming a Guardian in Prayer* (Bloomington, MN: Chosen Books, 2017), 57.

CHAPTER 6: COLLEGE DAYS

1. Babe Ruth Quotes, "Famous Quotes by Babe Ruth," BabeRuth.com, accessed June 26, 2017, http://www.baberuth.com/quotes/.

CHAPTER 7: TORRINGTON

1. Michael D. Sabock and Ralph J. Sabock, *Coaching: A Realistic Perspective*, 11th ed. (Lanham, MD: Rowman & Littlefield, 2017), 112.

CHAPTER 8: HIT-AND-RUN

1. Wayne Stewart, *The Gigantic Book of Baseball Quotations* (New York: Skyhorse, 2007), 452.
2. *Chariots of Fire*, film, directed by Hugh Hudson (Burbank, CA: Warner Bros., 1981).
3. John Nagowski, "Matters of Faith Sometimes Not That Far Afield," *Tallahassee Democrat*, May 26, 1998, C1.
4. Ibid.

CHAPTER 9: THE DRAFT

1. "All-Star Christian," beliefnet.com, accessed August 15, 2017, http://www.beliefnet.com/entertainment/celebrities/all-star -christian.aspx.
2. Kevin Sherrington, "Second Nature: Jason Benham Has Accepted Living in Baseball Shadow of Twin, David. Now, They Finally Go Separate Ways," *Dallas Morning News*, June 7, 1998, 24B. The full story is reprinted as the appendix.
3. Ibid.
4. See Genesis 25:21–26 and ch. 48.
5. Sherrington, "Second Nature."

CHAPTER 10: A RED SOX ROOKIE

1. Will McDonough, "A Scouting Mission for Moakley," *Boston Globe*, December 13, 1997, G1.

CHAPTER 11: BLUEFIELD BASEBAL

1. Jeffrey Scholes and Raphael Sassower, *Religion and Sports in American Culture* (New York: Routledge, 2014), 121.

CHAPTER 12: MEET ME IN ST. LOUIE

1. Paul Dickson, *Baseball's Greatest Quotations* (New York: Collins, 2008), 54.

CHAPTER 13: BROKEN

1. William J. Bennett and John T. E. Cribb, *The American Patriot's Almanac* (Nashville: Thomas Nelson, 2008), April 8.

CHAPTER 14: DYING TO THE DREAM

1. Vince Lombardi and Vince Lombardi Jr., *What It Takes to Be Number One* (Nashville: Thomas Nelson, 2012), 31.

CHAPTER 15: A SUMMER VISIT

1. Dr. Purushothaman, *Words of Wisdom: 1,001 Motivational and Inspirational Quotes*, vol. 24 (Kollam, India: Centre for Human Perfection, 2014), 46.

CHAPTER 16: HOME RUN DERBY

1. Tony Castro, *DiMag & Mick: Sibling Rivals, Yankee Blood Brothers* (Guilford, CT: Lyons Press, 2016), 127.

CHAPTER 17: A CRAZY IDEA

1. Paul Dickson, *Baseball's Greatest Quotations* (New York: Collins, 2008), 474.

CHAPTER 18: A NEW DAY

1. Paul Dickson, *Baseball's Greatest Quotations* (New York: Collins, 2008), 196.

CHAPTER 19: BREAK IT UP

1. Paul Dickson, *Baseball's Greatest Quotations* (New York: Collins, 2008), 592.

CHAPTER 20: SHREVEPORT

1. Tony Robbins, *Money: Master the Game* (New York: Simon and Schuster, 2014), 342.

ABOUT THE AUTHORS

David and Jason Benham are former professional baseball players, nationally acclaimed entrepreneurs, and bestselling authors of *Whatever the Cost* and *Living Among Lions*. The twin brothers' business success earned them a reality show with HGTV, set to air during the 2014 fall season. Due to their commitment to biblical values, however, the show was abruptly canceled. The Benhams immediately found themselves in the midst of a cultural firestorm, but they refused to back down and decided to stand and fight for what they believe.

The brothers' first company was recognized as one of *Inc.* magazine's Fastest Growing Private Companies, and they have been awarded Ernst & Young's Entrepreneur of the Year Finalists, *Wall Street Journal*'s Top Real Estate Professionals, and *Business Leader Media*'s Top 50 Entrepreneurs. They were also named *Franchise 500*'s Top New Franchise.

Appearing on CNN, Fox News, TheBlaze, ABC's *Nightline*, *Good Morning America*, and other media, the Benhams continue to stand up for what they believe and encourage others to do the same.

Both David and Jason are happily married, and their families live on the same street in Charlotte, North Carolina. Their wives, Lori and Tori, homeschool their combined nine children and are passionate about serving in their community.

Follow David and Jason on Twitter:
@BenhamBrothers
@DavidDBenham
@JasonBBenham
Visit their website, BenhamBrothers.com,
like them on Facebook/BenhamBrothers, and
follow them on Instagram/BenhamBrothers.

WHAT PEOPLE ARE SAYING ABOUT *WHATEVER THE COST*

"In *Whatever the Cost* the Benhams provide us with a living testimony of two guys who weren't afraid to speak out—no matter the cost. I know you'll enjoy their stories, but you also will be moved to display similar courage in standing for what is right."

—**MIKE HUCKABEE,** former Arkansas governor; host, *Huckabee,* Fox News; and bestselling author

"As an evangelist, my heart pounds when God's people proclaim the salvation message, and the Benhams do just that. This battle call will have you pick up your armor and fight, no matter the cost."

—**CHRISTINE CAINE,** founder, the A21 Campaign; and bestselling author, *Unstoppable*

"Amazing things happen when you keep your priorities straight. God. Family. Integrity. Financial wisdom. Generosity. These are the keys to winning, but too many people get it wrong and drive their whole lives off a cliff. In *Whatever the Cost,* David and Jason show you how to achieve incredible success by making God and family the cornerstones of your life."

—**DAVE RAMSEY,** *New York Times* bestselling author and nationally syndicated radio show host

978-0-7180-8317-5

DO YOU HAVE WHAT IT TAKES TO BE A MODERN-DAY DANIEL?

978-0-7180-7641-2

Discover what it takes to live victoriously in a world increasingly hostile to people of faith.

"When you have to live among the lions, the Benham brothers are the kinds of Christians you want as neighbors."

—**TODD STARNES,** Fox News Channel

"Rarely have I seen a more desperate time when we need courageous Christians to rise up. In *Living Among Lions* the Benham brothers provide a clear call."

—**DR. CHARLES STANLEY,** senior pastor, First Baptist Church, Atlanta

"As a mother of boys, I'm so grateful that the Benhams have chronicled their insight and personal legacy in these pages."

—**PRISCILLA SHIRER,** author and teacher